MORE WOODWORK PROJECTS

W. G. Alton

Senior Lecturer, Trent Park College of Education
with diagrams by the author

ALLMAN AND SON London
TAPLINGER PUBLISHING COMPANY New York

First published in England, 1969
by Allman and Son Limited
50 Grafton Way, Fitzroy Street, London, W1A 1DR
© W. G. Alton 1969
British SBN 204.74638.8
American SBN 8008-5370-9

First published in the United States in 1969 by
Taplinger Publishing Co Inc
29 East Tenth Street
New York, New York 10003
Library of Congress Catalog Card No
75-87082

By the same author
WOODWORK PROJECTS
METALWORK PROJECTS—FURNITURE

Phototypeset and printed in Great Britain by
BAS Printers Limited, Wallop, Hampshire

Contents

Glossary for American Readers

Technical woodworking terms vary in different localities. Consult the list here for synonyms and definitions where applicable.

Blockboard—solid-core plywood (two sheets of veneer separated by strips of wood rather than by sheets of coring).

Bridle Joint—a kind of rabbet joint.

Comb Joint—a kind of mortise-and-tenon joint (may also substitute for dovetail).

Cotton Reel—cotton spool, for thread.

Draughts—checkers (the game).

Fall—drop-leaf.

Fittings—hardware.

Foam—foam rubber.

Folio—large-size drawing paper, about 22 inches by 30 inches.

G Cramp—C clamp.

Jig Cramp—jig clamp.

Laminboard—laminated board, a solid-core plywood (see *Blockboard* above) with double sheets of veneer on each side.

Lino—linoleum.

Lipping—edge-banding (finish stripping applied to the ragged edge of plywood to make it appear a solid piece). Stripping can be from $\frac{3}{16}$ inch thick up to $\frac{5}{8}$ inches thick. It is applied by glue or screws.

Pins—thin gauge nails, veneer pins.

P.V.C.—plastic material (from *polyvinylchloride*).

Rabet—rabbet, a kind of joint.

Resin W—trade name for *Resin Glue*.

Sellotape—pressure sensitive tape.

Slips—strips of wood.

Spanner—wrench.

Zips—zippers.

Preface

It is felt that ambitious pieces of furniture may often not be attempted because of the risk involved in the general conception, use of material and selection of techniques.

This book endeavours to bring together modern materials and methods of construction associated with them. It would be a pity if, for a lack of an idea or technique, the making of a piece of furniture was not attempted. It is hoped that sufficient ideas have been shown and sufficient basic measurements indicated to give a lead. It is hoped even more that craftsmen involved will think out their own basic requirements and adapt and modify accordingly.

The drawings in this book have been made as clear as possible and should be self-explanatory. In some cases technical terms may be confusing, since words vary in different localities. It would be advisable for the reader to become familiar with the glossary on the preceding page before reading the instructions.

W.G.A.

Drawing-writing Table 1

This table has three main features—a lift-up top, storage for paper and folio and an attached box with hinged lid and sliding tray for the instruments. 27″ is a comfortable working height but the height should be decided by individual requirements. The centre frame is made large enough to easily hold an imperial-size folio. It can be made from 3″ × 1″ and the corner joints can be comb, through dovetail or stopped dovetail. The back and front should be rebated for plywood but it can be overlaid on the sides.

The drawing board is made from $\frac{5}{8}$″ blockboard and the lipping can be mitred at the corners. If Resin W is used the lipping can be glued straight on to the blockboard edge. The board can be veneered, painted or covered with plastic laminate or lino, in which last case the edges will have to be protected with lipping after fixing the lino with a fairly thick application of Resin W adhesive.

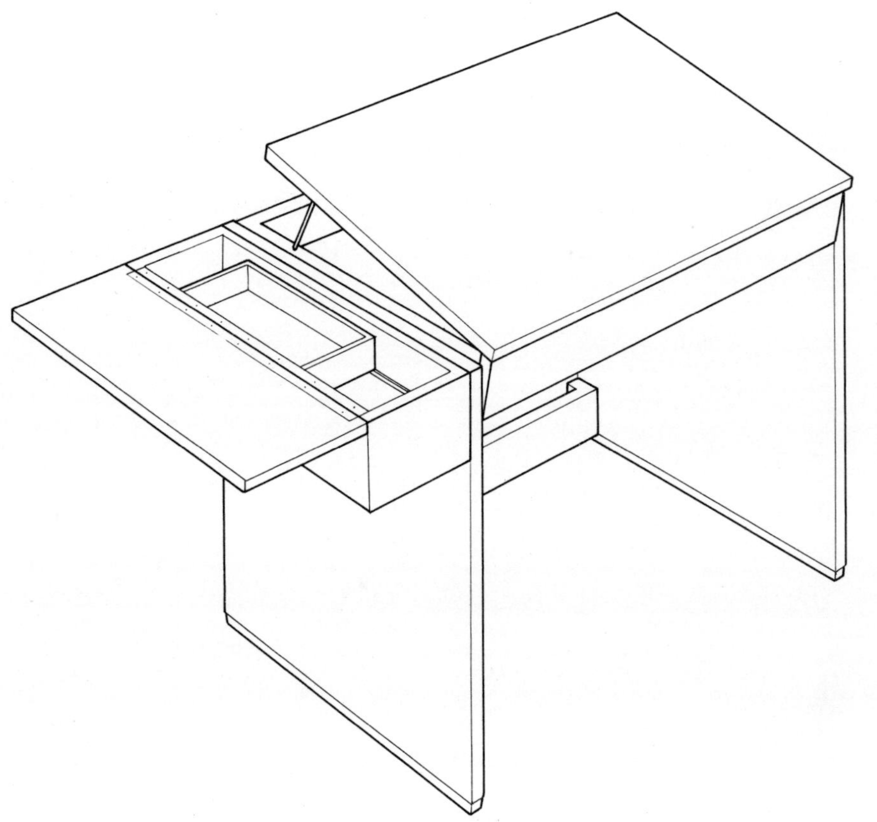

If a plastic laminate is used then a sheet of paper
under the drawing sheet will give better compass
point location.
The front face of the drawing board is secured by
locating with dowels and gluing. The butt hinges or
piano hinge is laid on to both the inner front face
and the frame, thus providing a clearance between
the surfaces.
The side panels are lipped sheets of $\frac{5}{8}$" blockboard
and can be veneered or painted and are secured to
the centre frame by bolts or screws and glue. They
must be located so that the tee square can slide
without interference. Unlipped $\frac{5}{8}$" plywood can
also be used.

1   Lap dovetail at back of centre frame.

2   Hinge movement.

3   Comb joint on front of frame.

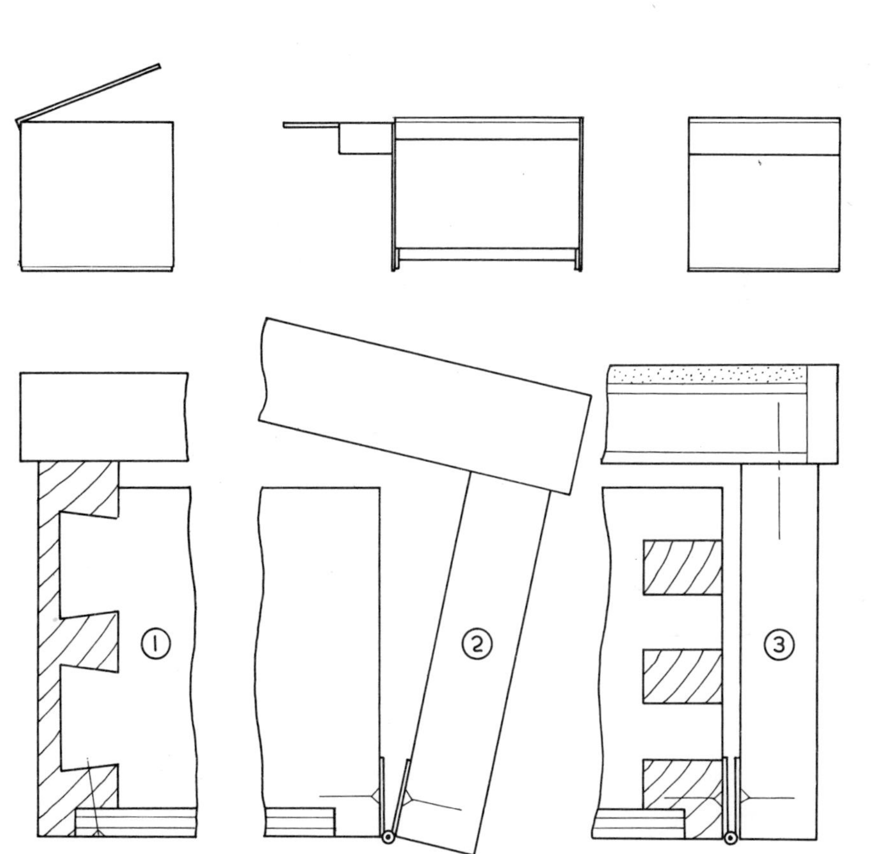

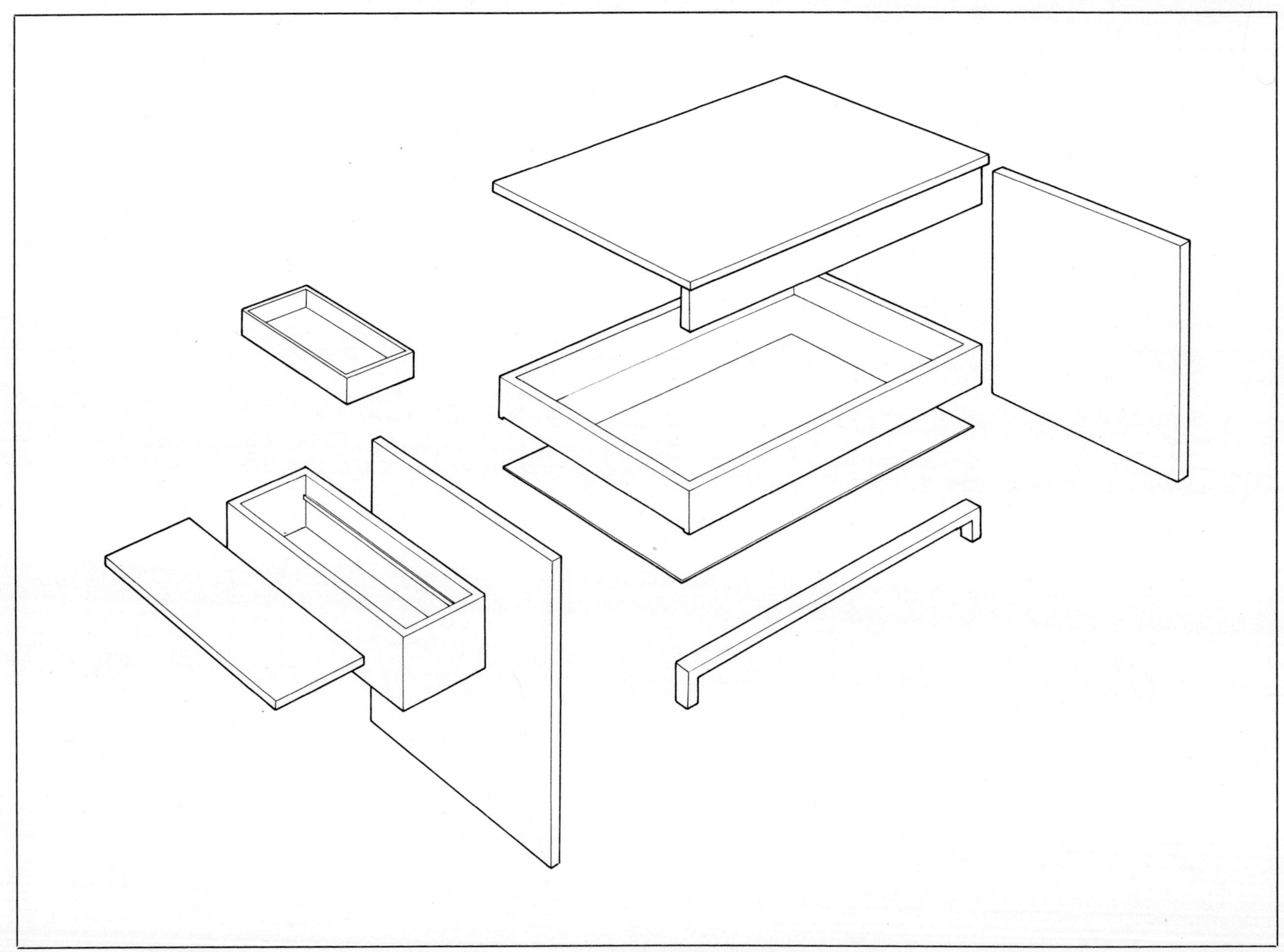

The inclination of the board is obtained by inserting two 6″ pieces of $\frac{5}{16}$″ dowel into holes.
The drawing instrument box can be made from $\frac{1}{2}$″ or $\frac{5}{8}$″ material. Joints on the outer corners could be secret mitre dovetails and lap dovetails on the inner corners. The plywood bottom can be rebated in. The box top would be made from veneered blockboard and if a continuous surface is required between the top of the box and the drawing board then thicknesses must be similar.

4 Secret mitre dovetail for box.

5 Lap dovetail for box.

6 Through dovetail for tray.

7 $\frac{5}{16}$″ dowel strut for tilting drawing board.

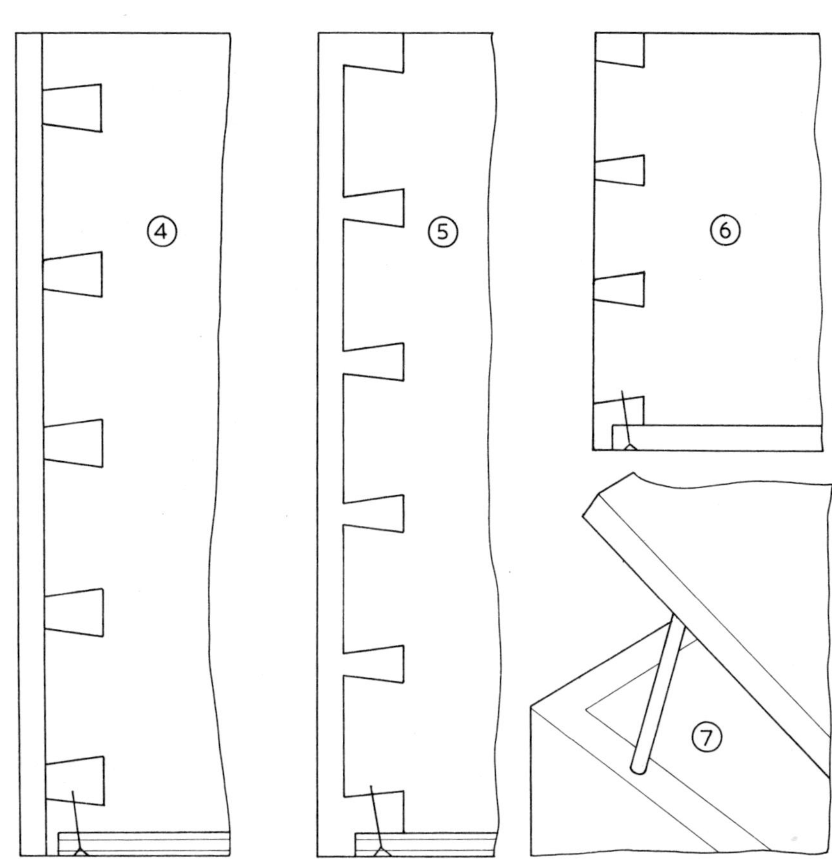

8 Box lid closed.

9 Section through instrument box and tray.

10 Butt hinge fitted between box and lid.

11 Butt hinge socket cut in box.

12 Piano hinge fitted between box and lid
   (alternative)

13 Piano hinge socket cut in box.

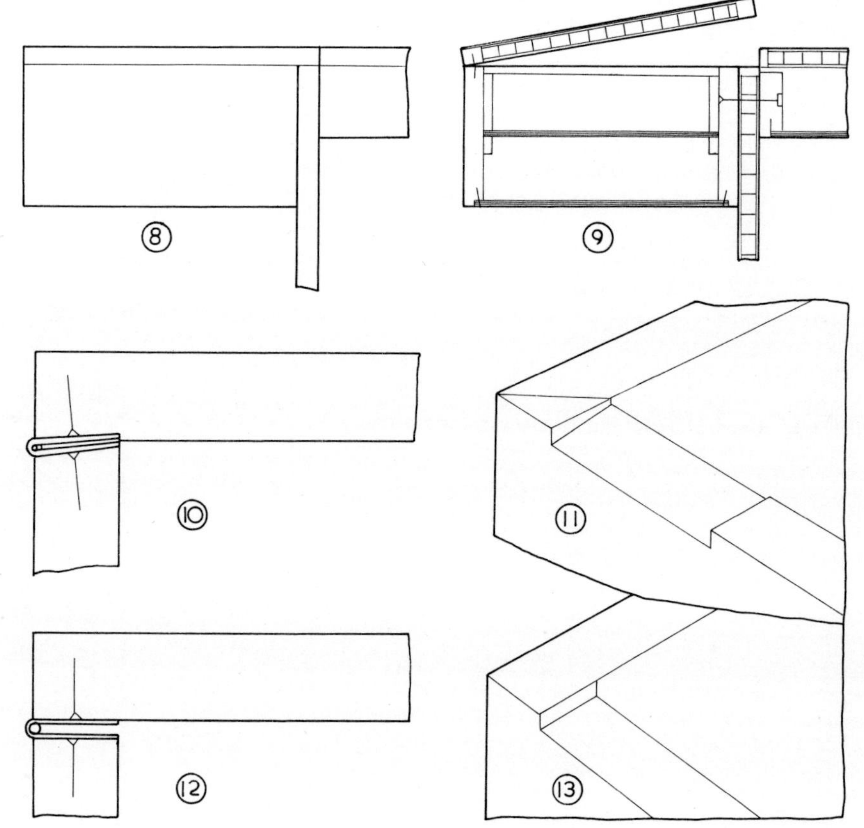

The lower back rail is made with end pieces to
provide greater strength through a larger gluing
area than would be possible with a stopped mortise
and tenon joint. Alternatively a square brass nut
can be inserted in the rail and a $\frac{1}{4}''$ brass or nickel
plated countersunk screw passed through the panel.
A pleasant contrast can be obtained with painted
panels and other parts finished with precatalysed
lacquer showing natural wood.

14, 15   Alternative forms of rail and wooden blocks.

16   Location of nut in rail.

17   Location of dowel and bolt in rail.

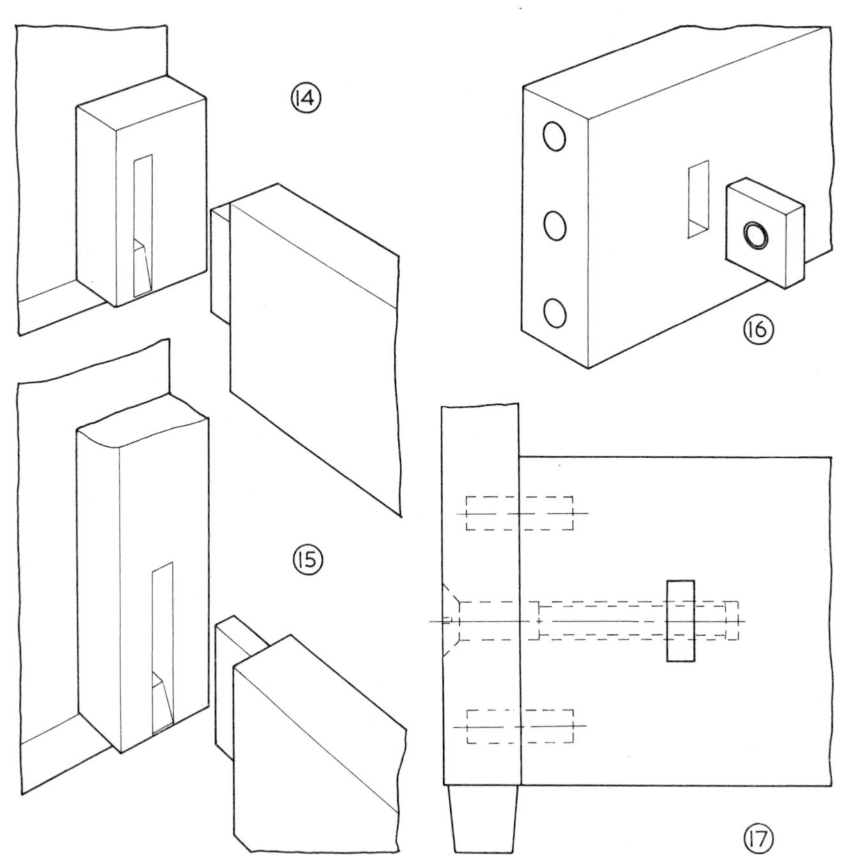

Drawing-writing Table 2

The main features of this table are a lift-up drawing board, storage for a half imperial folio and paper, instrument storage with sliding tray and a drawer. A very satisfactory working height is 27" but this must be decided by the user. The size of the storage must be based on a half imperial folder which should fit easily with about an inch to spare all round. 3" × 1" would be satisfactory for the rails and $1\frac{3}{4}$" × $1\frac{1}{8}$" for legs would make a rigid structure. The ply bottom can be set in a groove or rebate in which case it can be in one or two pieces—the join being on the partition. The ply bottom can be set into the legs for $\frac{1}{8}$" or cut round as preferred. If the ply is let into a groove it must of course be set in when the table is glued together. If the ply is rebated it can be let in after gluing, but if the ply is rebated and set in the legs then it must be made in two halves and offered in separately, both being screwed onto the partition.

The drawing board, which is made from $\frac{3}{8}$" blockboard, can be finished in a variety of ways. A $\frac{3}{8}$" lipping can be glued on using Resin W and the board left in the white or painted. It may be covered with plastic laminate or lino, in which case it should be lipped after the lino is glued.

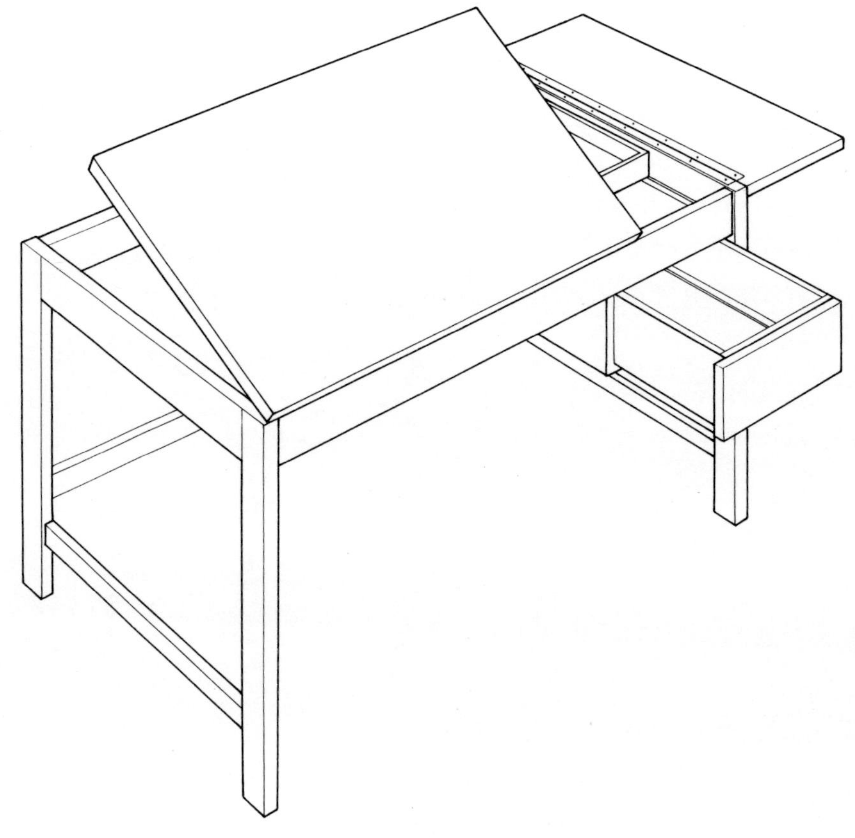

1 Leg, rails and ply assembly.

2 Leg, rails and ply joints.

3 Plan details of leg, rails and ply assembly.

4 Vertical section through rail and partition
   showing ply in groove.

5 Vertical section through rail and partition
   showing ply in rebate.

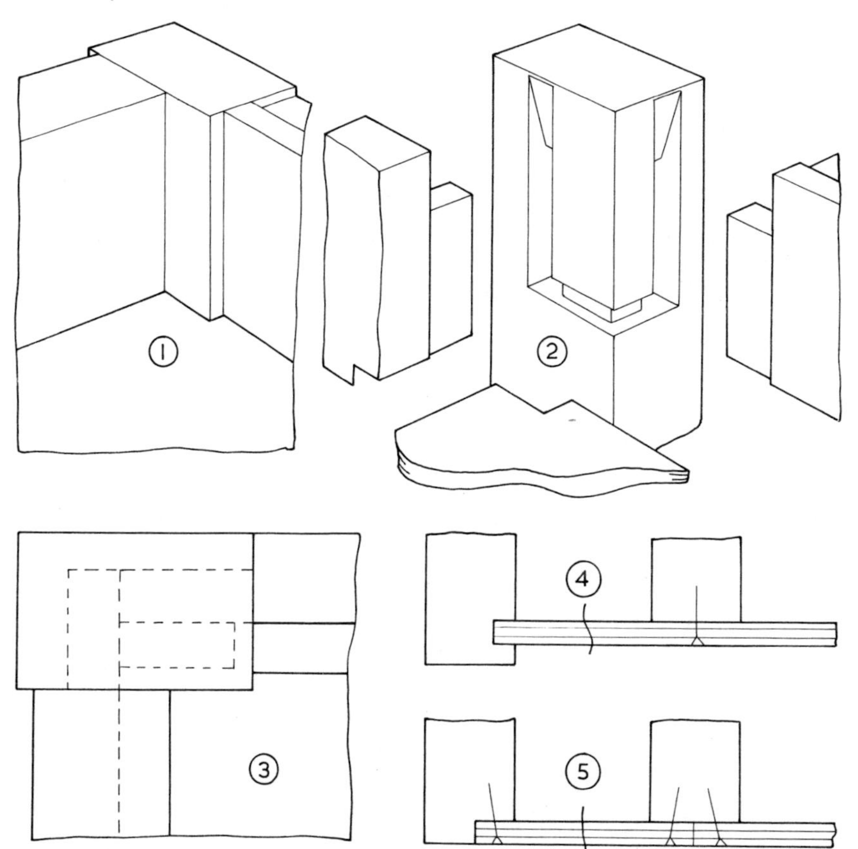

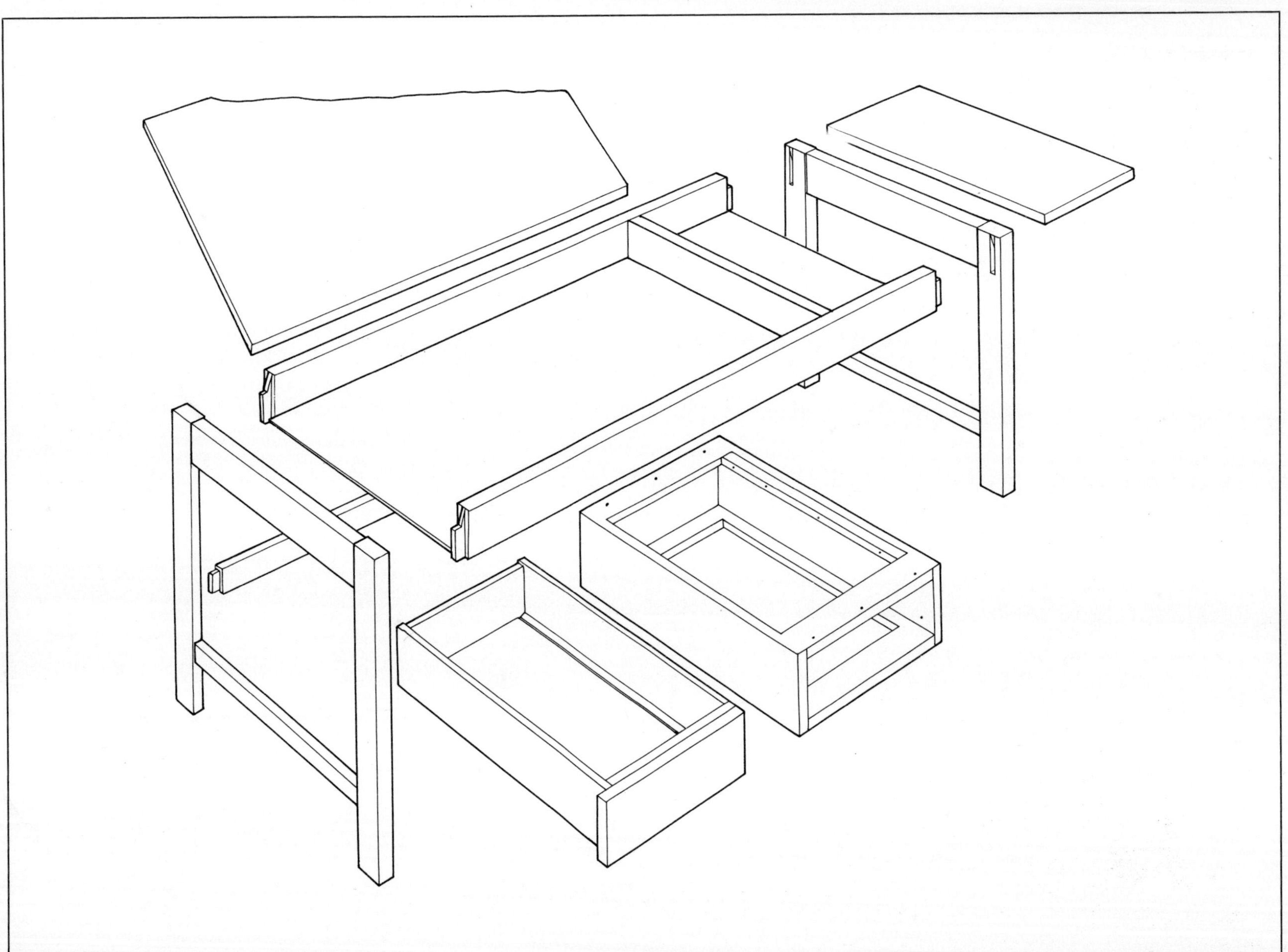

Two butt hinges can be used for securing the drawing board to the underframe. The instrument box top should finish at the same level as the drawing board. The top can be hinged with a $1\frac{1}{4}$" piano hinge or butt hinges. If the drawing board and top are in line with the legs at the back, then $\frac{1}{8}$" overhang will be sufficient for opening both.
The angle of the drawing board can be set with two pieces of $\frac{1}{4}$" diameter bright mild steel framed as shown. A variety of angles may be obtained by setting in other pairs of holes.

 6 Stub tenon and housing on partition.

 7 Stub tenon in lower rail.

 8 Arm for setting angle of drawing board.

 9 Arm.

10 Setting butt hinge on drawing board.

11 Setting piano hinge on instrument box lid.

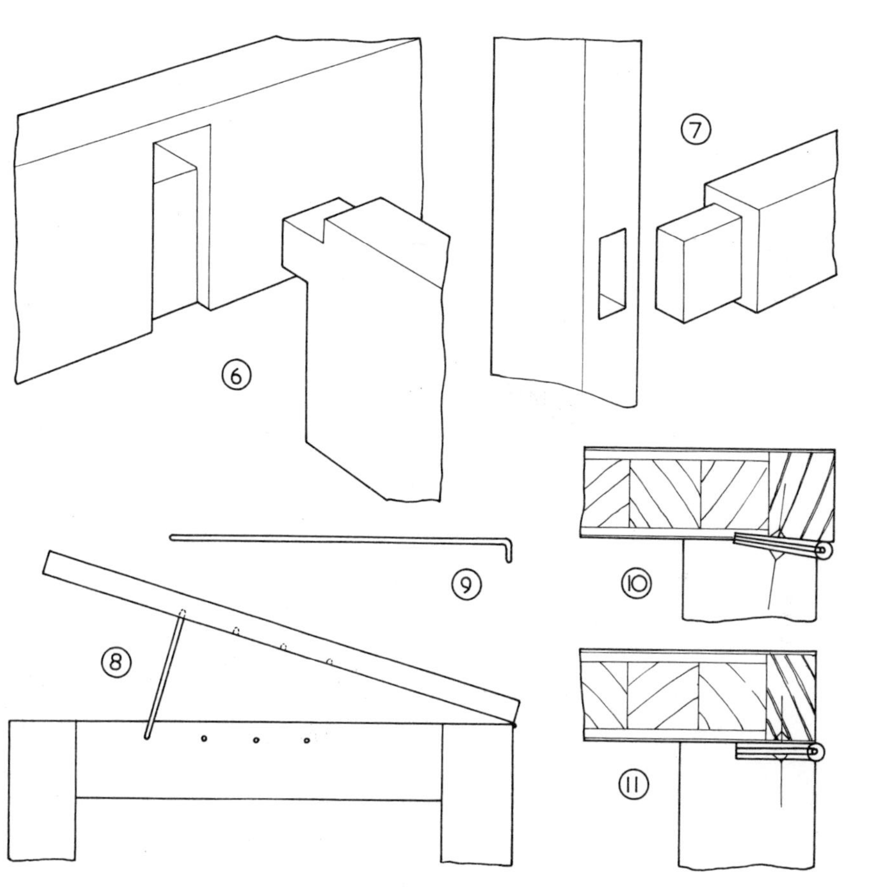

The drawer box sides are made from $\frac{5}{8}$ " blockboard
which can be lipped at the top and bottom and
battened at the ends as shown. Alternatively a
blockboard side can be used with thin front and
back lippings only, in which case the blocks of the
board should run vertically and the cross rail pin
sockets should be as wide as the dovetails to
prevent breaking out. The sides are veneered on
both sides.
The rear ply panel can be slid into the box from the
top. Grooves would be made on two sides and the
bottom. Kicker rails and drawer runners can be
glued and screwed in before or after the box is
glued together.

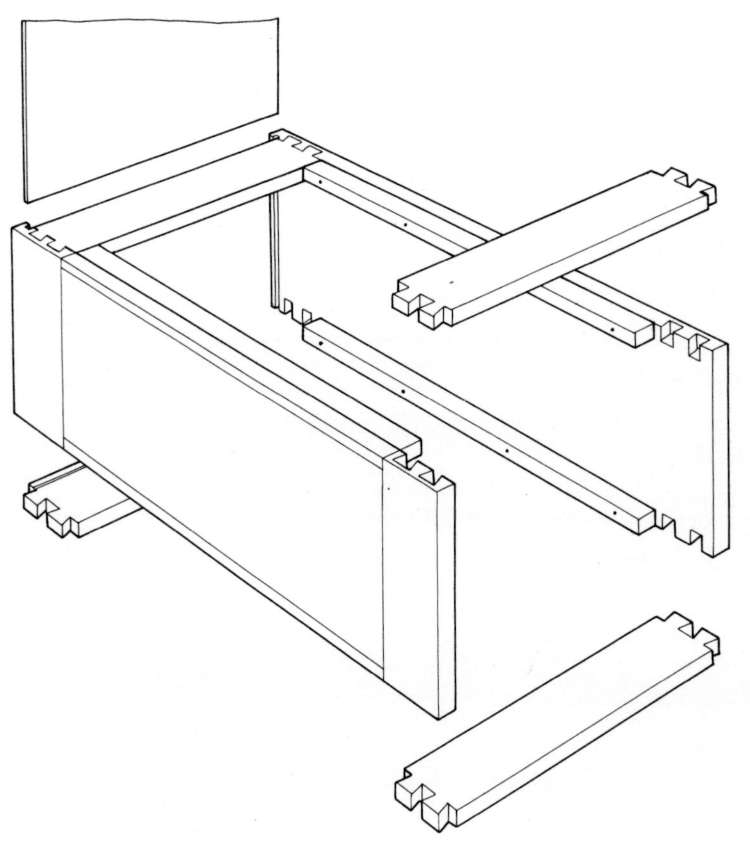

The $\frac{3}{8}$" drawer material is cut and fitted into the box
and after jointing and gluing together the $\frac{1}{2}$" front
is laid on by screwing for location and gluing. The
ply is grooved into the inside of the front and into
slips which are glued on to the sides.

DRAWER

12 Through dovetails (front). Front laid on.

13 Back dovetails.

14 Section through side showing slips and ply.

15 Back of drawer.

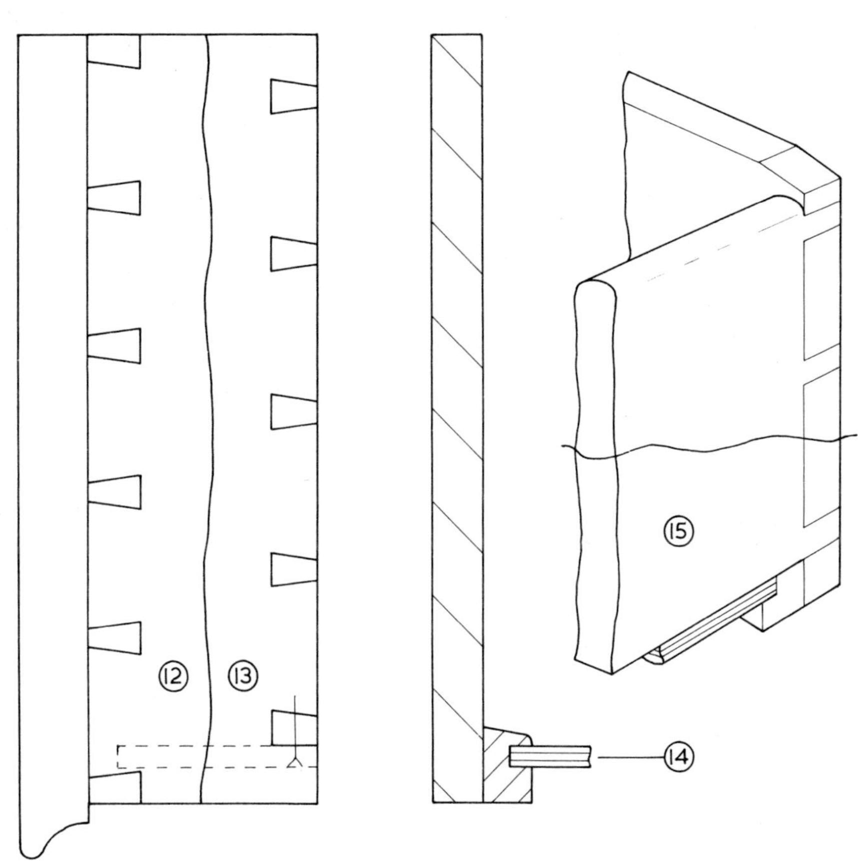

17

Armchair

This is an inexpensive easily made chair. The British standard for minimum inside width for a chair with arms is 19″ but an extra inch or so will improve the function and the appearance. The inside height of the back cushion is 18″ but this could be more if required. The seat can be 22″ front to back but again this can be varied. The height of the front edge of the seat cushion is 16″ and the height of the arm rest can be 20″–23″. It is a sound plan to sit in some chairs and then measure them and work out your own requirements. Likewise, the side panels can be shaped in a variety of ways. These are made from $\frac{1}{2}$″ or $\frac{5}{8}$″ blockboard or multiply. If made from blockboard the front and back edges will require lipping. This can be applied directly using Resin W as an adhesive.

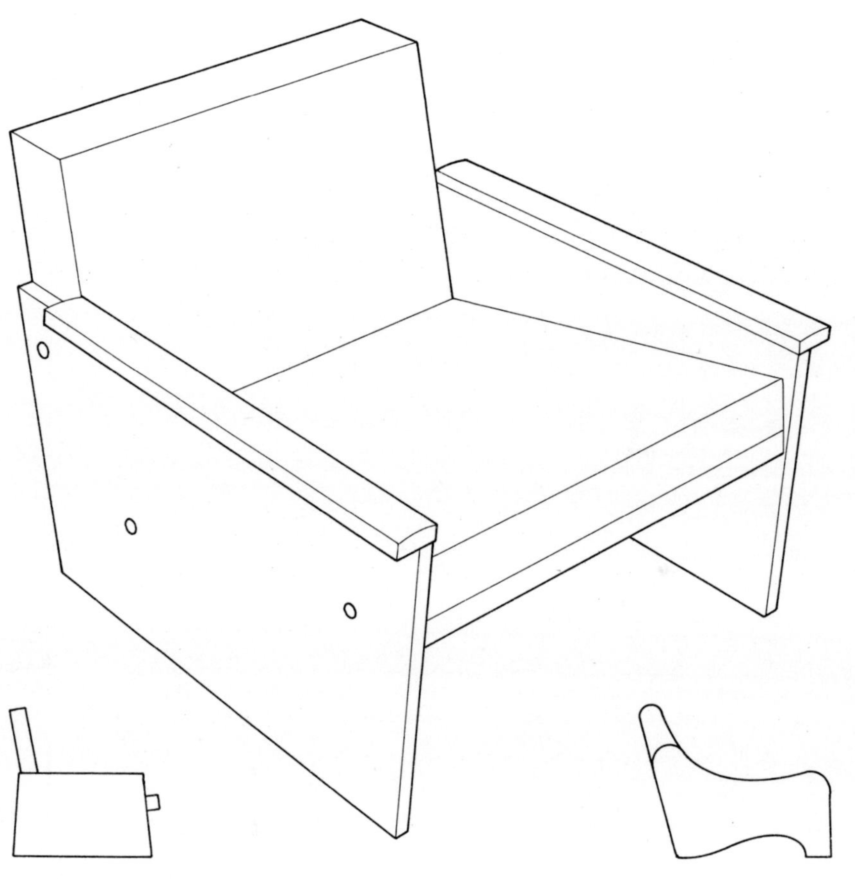

The corners on the lower edges must be rounded a little to lessen the risk of splitting. The top edge at the back will require a short lipping or edge filling. The surfaces are filled and painted. White will make a striking contrast with the upholstery material and acrylic emulsion paint is easy to apply, gives a tough washable finish and the brushes are easily cleaned in water. Polyurethane paint may also be used.

1   Comb joint for seat frame.

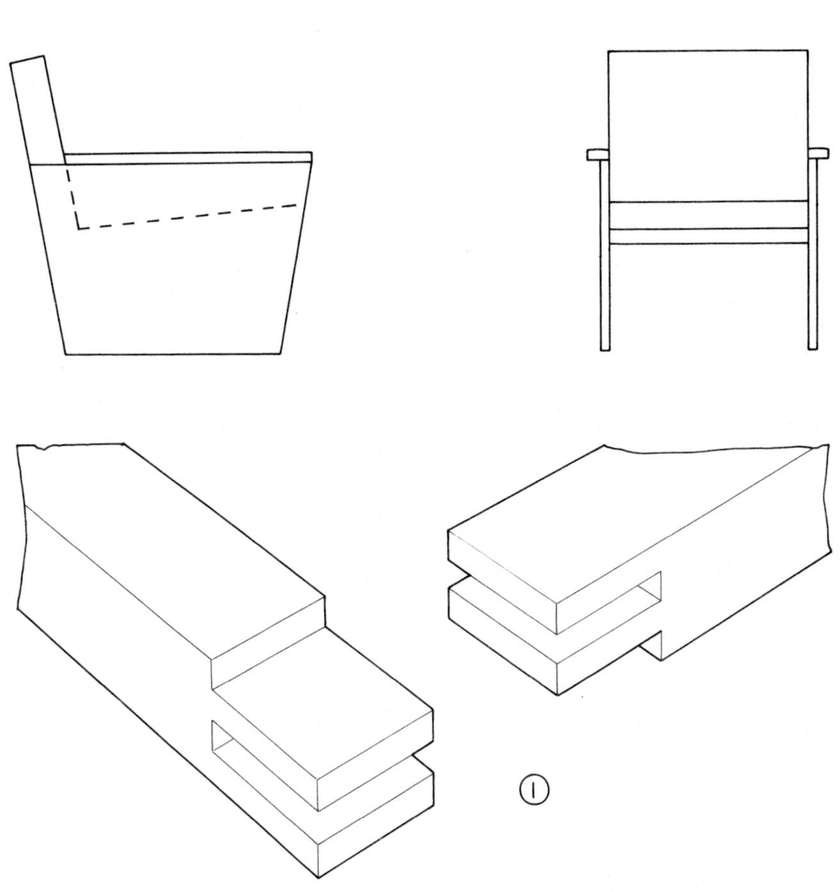

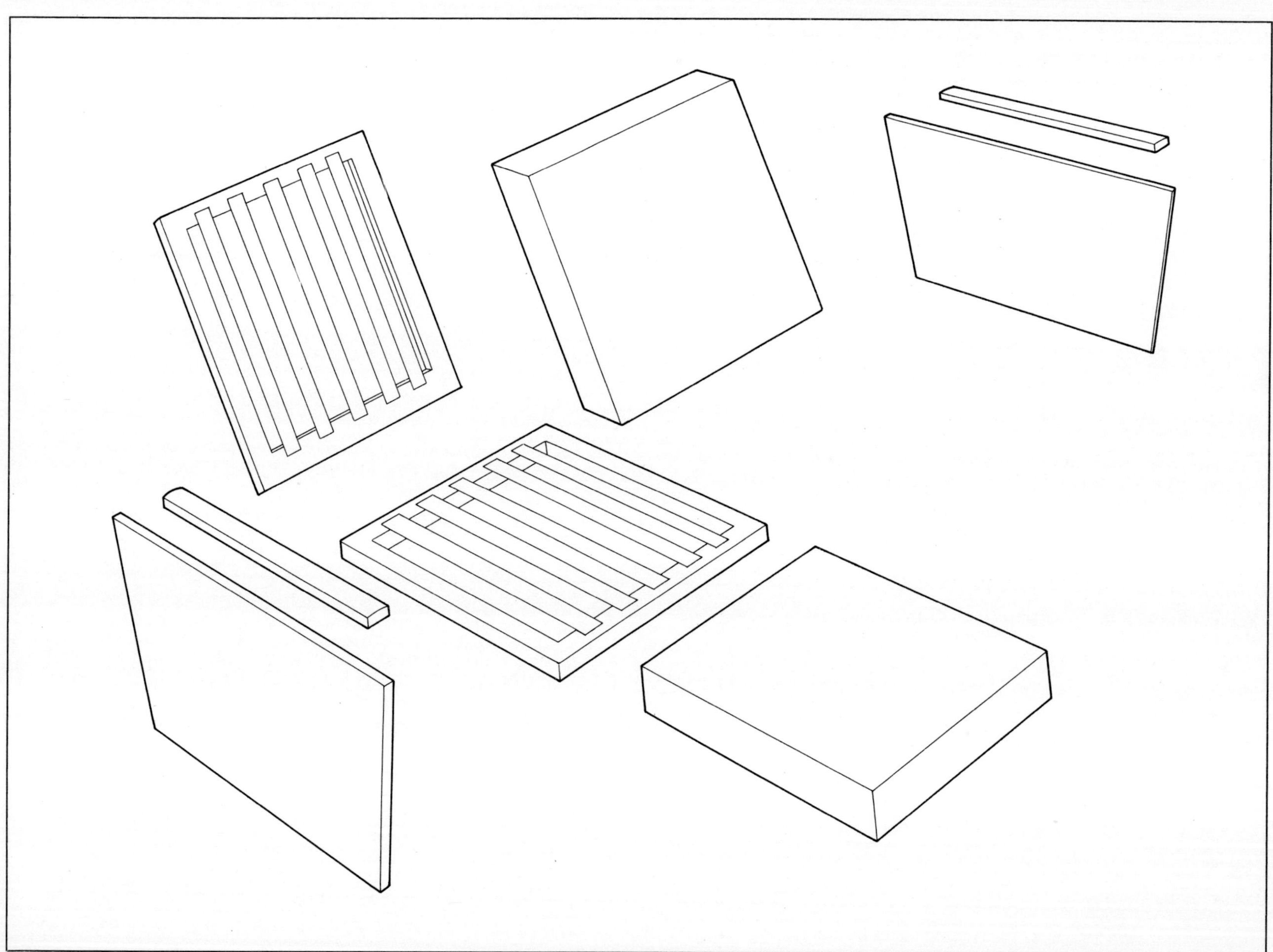

The seat and back medium density plastic foam
cushions are supported on 2″ rubber webbing
tacked on the wooden frames, which are screwed
or bolted to each other and also to the side panels.
The heads of the bolts in the side panels can be
featured, especially if made from brass, otherwise
they can be set in counterdrilled holes and fitted
flush or featured with a plug. The arms can be
dowelled and secured using Resin W adhesive.

2 Back and seat frames joined together. 2″ rubber
   webbing tacked on.

3 Fastenings between side panels and frame.

4 Arm rest.

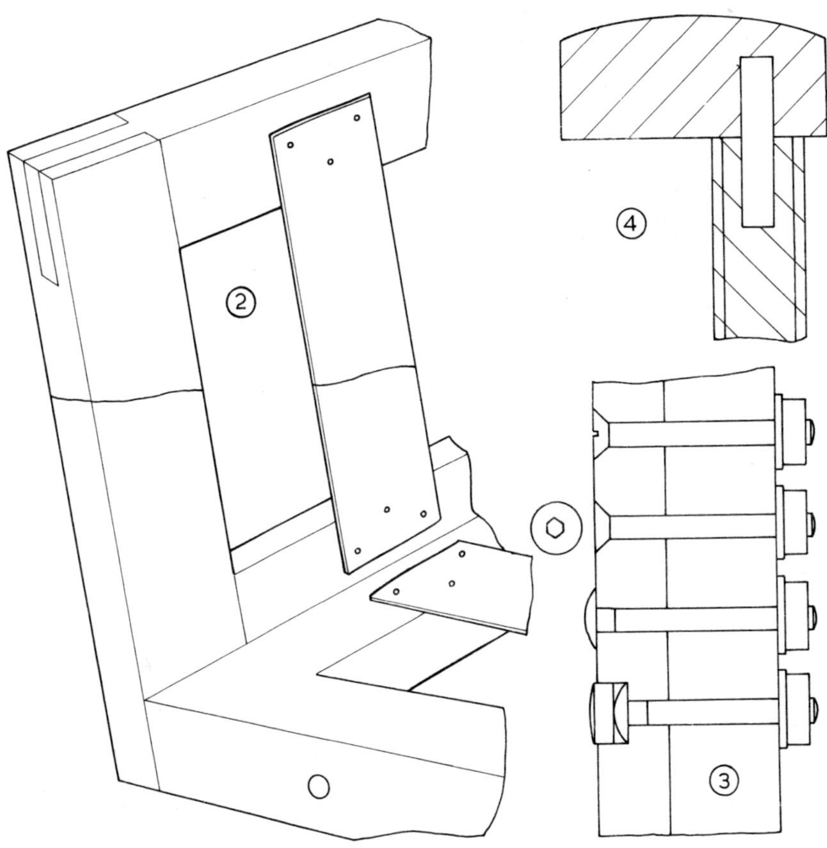

There are two different ways to upholster. The cushions can be completely covered, with zips fitted if required, and if a zip is fitted then the foam cushion can be entered easily ; otherwise it will be necessary to leave one edge unstitched until the foam is in place. With this method the back frame is covered before the frames are bolted to the side panels.

5 Joint on back (or mortise and tenon).

6 Material cut ready for tacking.

7 Material tacked down on inside of frame.

8 Covered cushion in place.

The other method is to upholster the foam in place
on the seat and back by simply boxing it round.
The corners may be machine stitched or hand
stitched after the material has been tacked down.
If P.V.C. is used, machine stitching from the inside
is desirable. A piece of material is now cut for the
back with sufficient extra ($\frac{5}{8}$″) for turning under all
round. This is nailed or stapled along the top edge
(underside) and is then pulled over and finally
nailed into position. Small headed gimp pins are
best for finally tacking down the back.

REAR VIEWS OF BACK FRAME

 9 Foam set on frame.

10 Material placed over frame.

11 Material nailed and sewn in place.

12 Back material nailed on before being dropped
     into place.

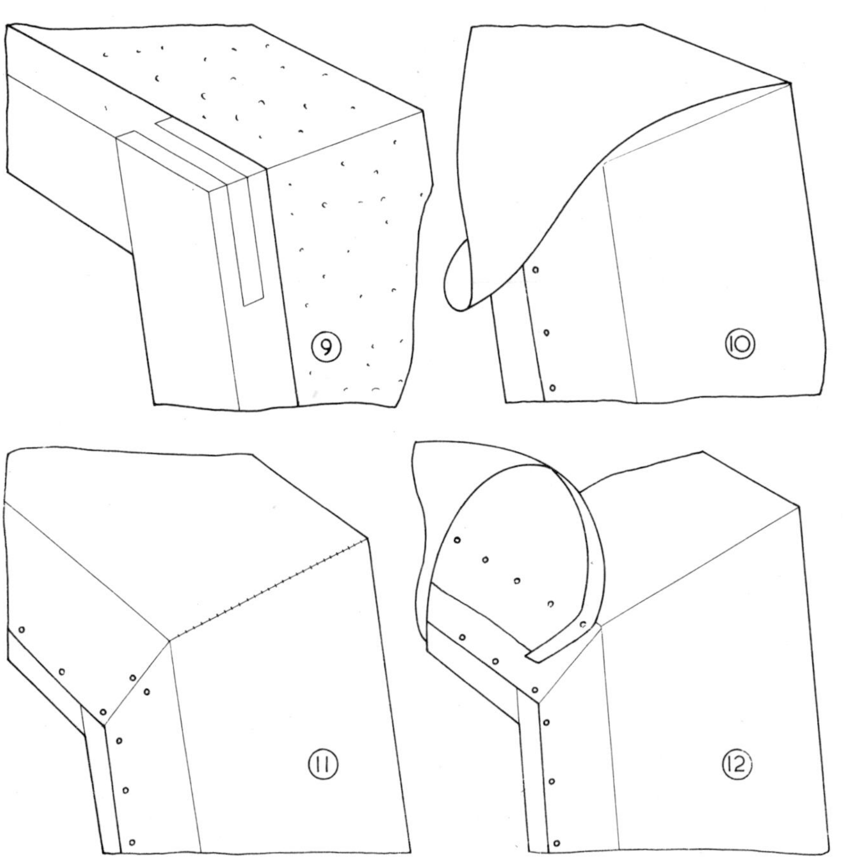

Settee and Easy Chairs

These can be made from a good grade red pine or other wood and then lacquered or painted with a tough washable acrylic emulsion or polyurethane paint. Coloured printed cotton upholstery would make a lively contrast with white paint.
SETTEE The legs are made from 3″ × 1½″ material and the front top edge of the 3″ polyether foam seat is 15″ above floor level. The side rails are made from 6″ × 1¼″ or 1″ material. The seat from front to back is 25″ (although more or less may be preferred) but as the 3″ thick foam back overlaps the seat the actual seating distance is only 22″. The height of the back cushion is 18″ but this of course could be more or less depending on individual requirements. The length of the cushion can be 48″ or as required, and the long rails can be 3″ × 1½″ material. The edges of all members should be well rounded. The long rails can be fixed to the end frames by mortise and tenon, ½″ dowels, 3″ × ¼″ bolts or metal screws. If hexagonal bolts are used then the counterdrilled holes should be large enough to take a box spanner. Bolt heads or counterdrillings can be painted or filled with dowel

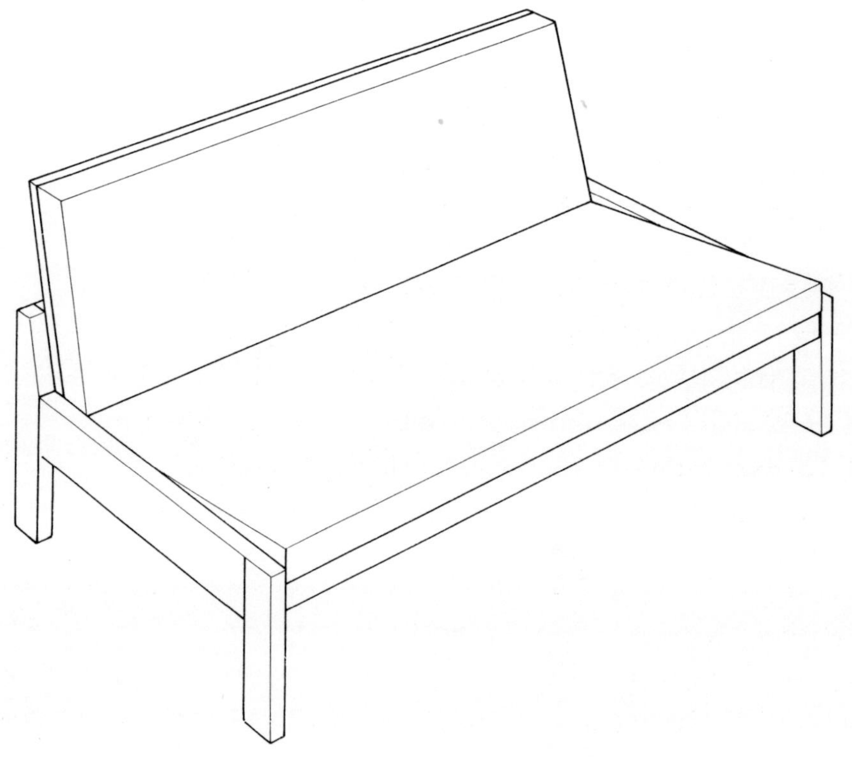

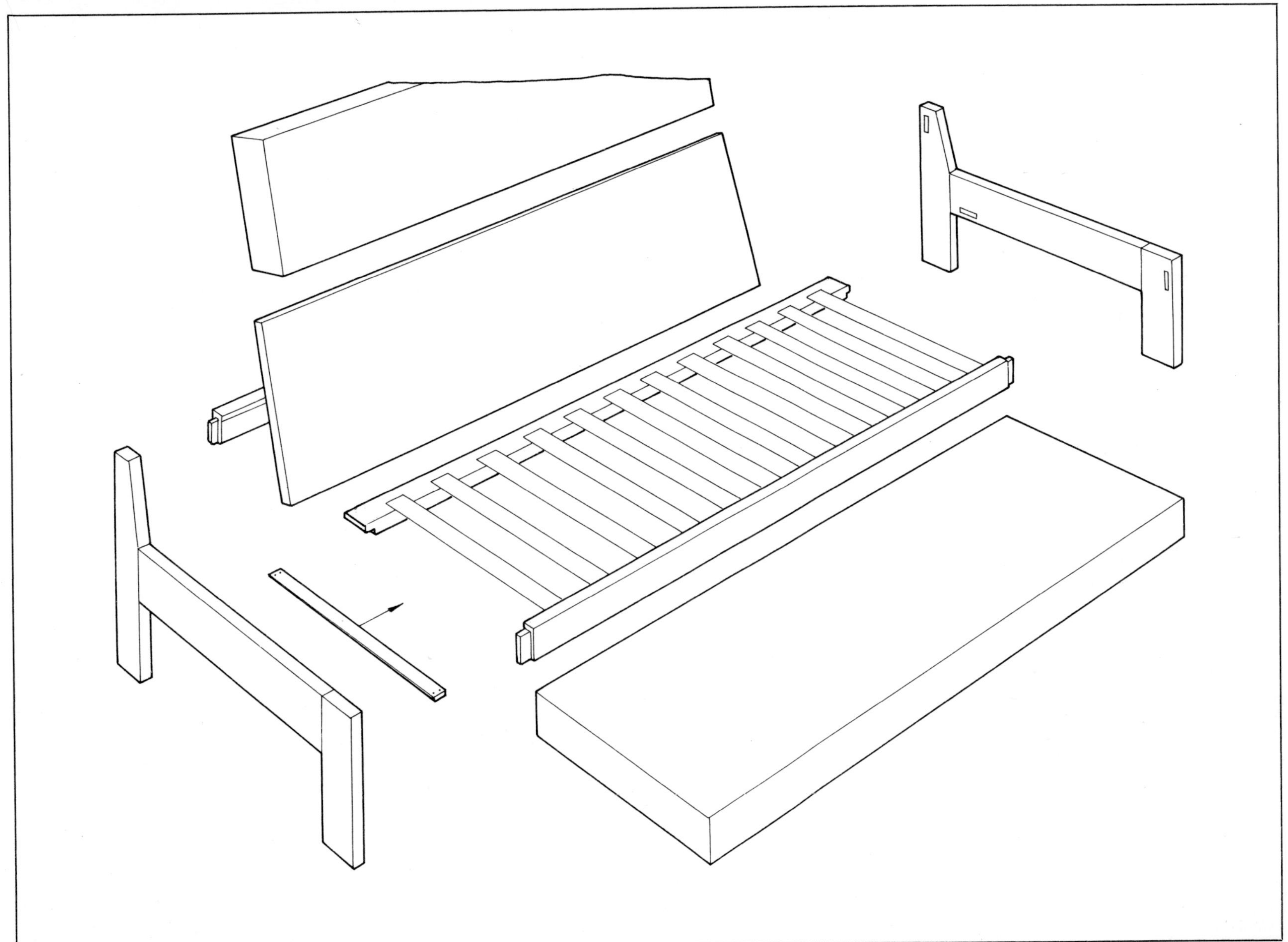

buttons slightly above the surface. A jig made from a
piece of $\frac{3}{16}$" or $\frac{1}{4}$" plate to a length of 2" × 2" L
section angle iron would be useful for drilling $\frac{1}{4}$"
holes for bolts or $\frac{1}{2}$" holes for dowels. An extra $\frac{1}{8}$"
plate used as a spacer will offset the holes by $\frac{1}{8}$"
where a shoulder is required at the joint. The back
board can be $\frac{1}{2}$" blockboard or ply with the edges
lipped or filled. Alternatively this surface can be
covered in material before fitting into place. The
seat rests on 2" rubber webbing which can be
nailed on to the rails or secured by clips fixed into
grooves. The webbing is stretched $1\frac{1}{4}$"–$1\frac{1}{2}$" for
each 10" of span. If it is found to be too flexible then
one or two webbings may be woven through and
secured by tacking to small battens on the side rails.
To prevent the side rails from pulling in, a 1" × $\frac{1}{4}$"
steel strut is screwed in the middle to the undersides.
Arms of 2" × $1\frac{1}{2}$" material can be fitted if required
and for this purpose the front leg would be made
the same length as the back leg.
The covers can be made from a variety of materials.
A strong 36" zip sewn into the back makes the
cleaning easier.

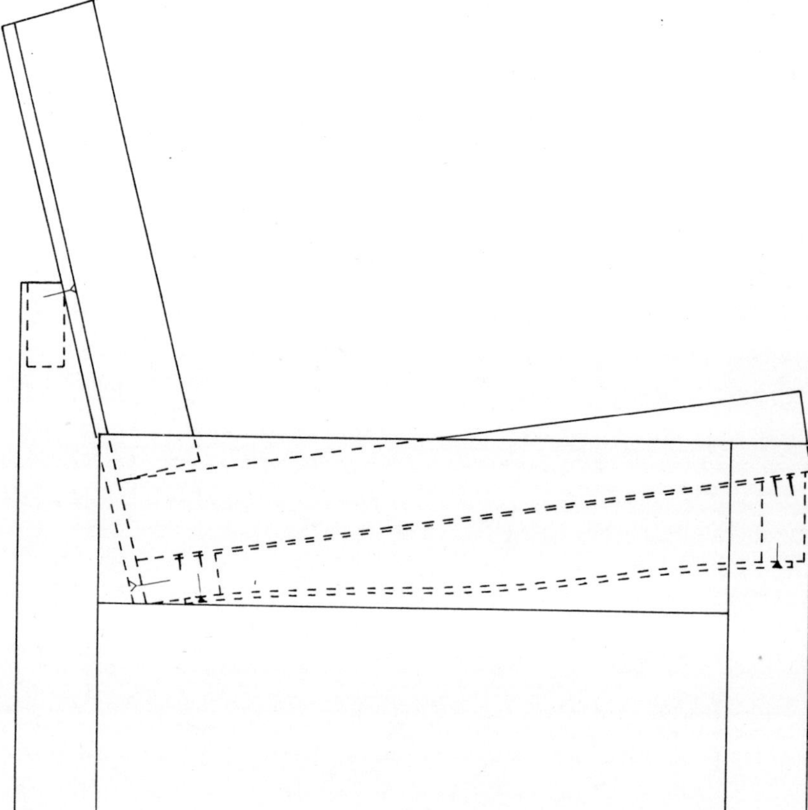

1 Elevation of front rail bolted to end frame.

2 Plan of front rail bolted to end frame.

3 Nut and socket.

4 Steel jig cramped on to rail for drilling.

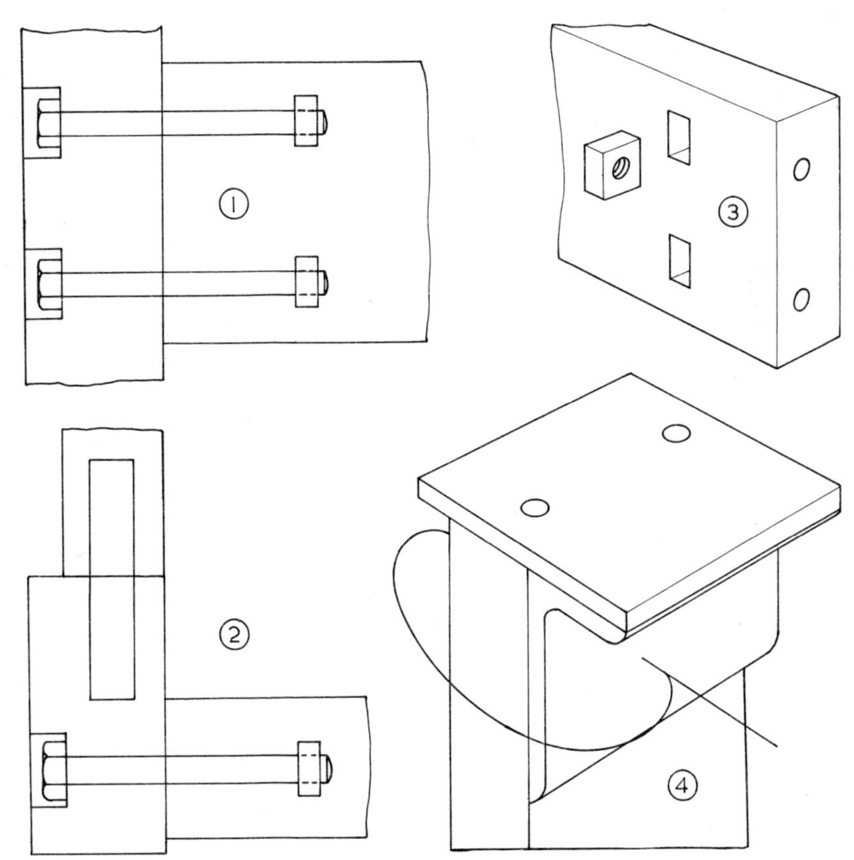

5 Metal countersunk screws as an alternative to
   hexagonal bolts.

6 $\frac{1}{2}$" dowel joints for main frames as an alternative
   to mortise and tenon joints.

7 Mortise and tenon joints on frames.

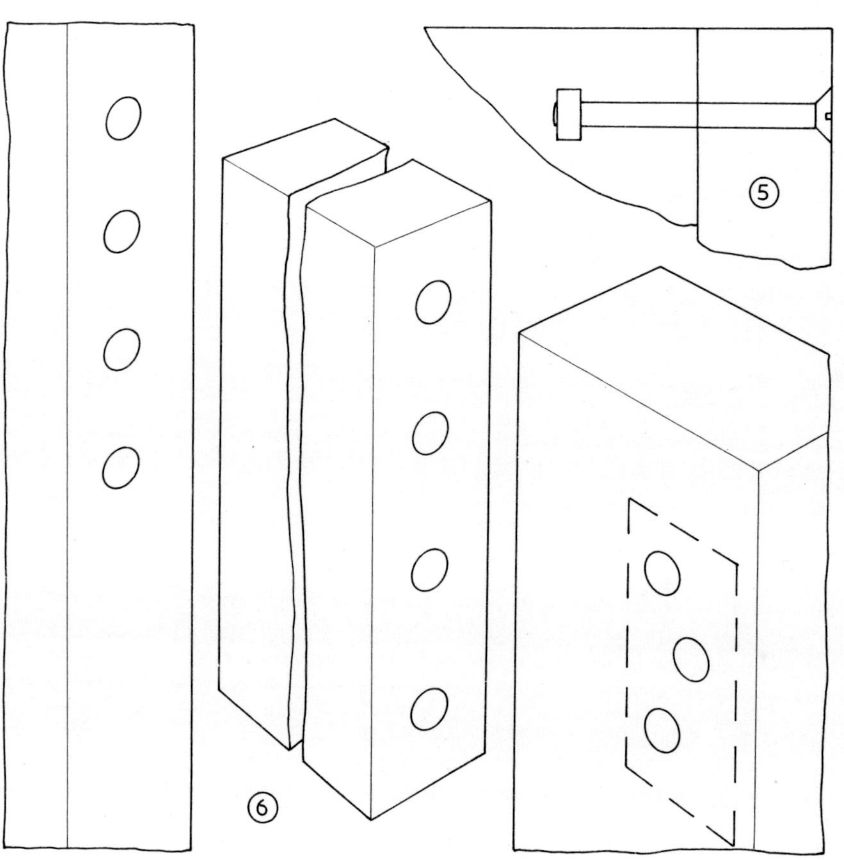

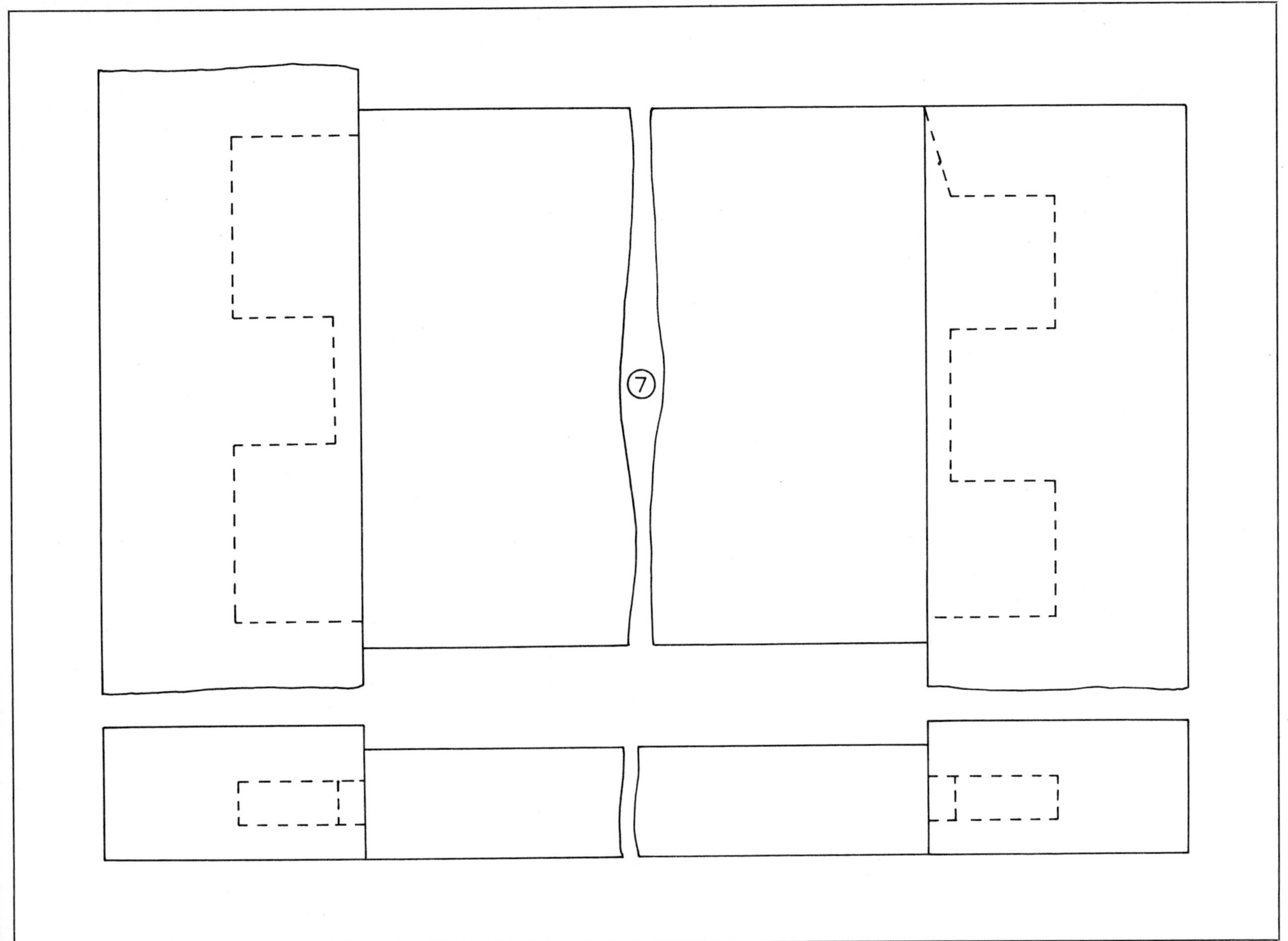

⑦

8 Rubber webbing tacked on.

9 Rubber webbing in clips in grooves.

10 Rubber webbing clip.

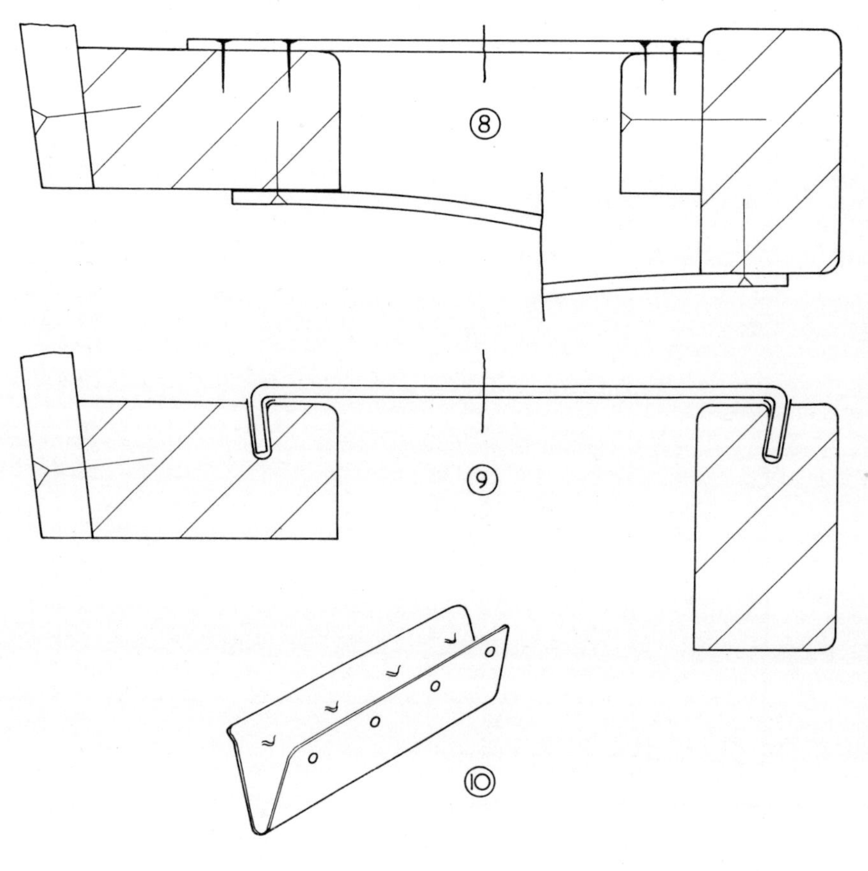

Chair

This will be made in a similar way but the legs can be made from $1\frac{1}{4}''$ and the rails from $1''$ material. The centre cross rail which is fitted on the settee to resist the pulling of the webbing is now unnecessary.

11 Back rail—alternative fitting.

12 Arm rest joints (if required).

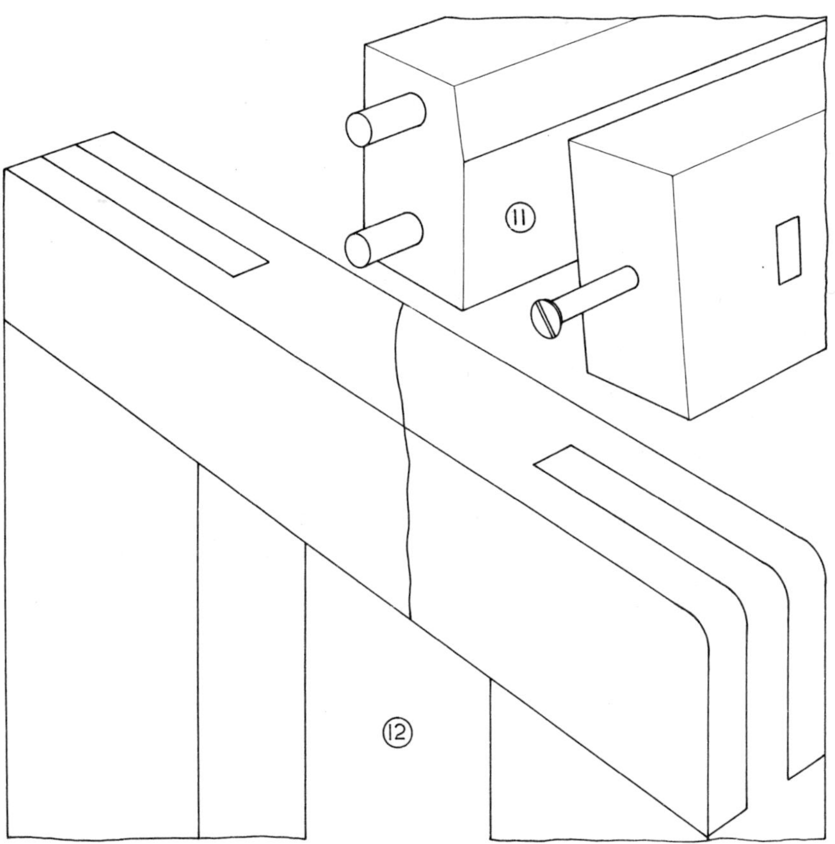

Rocking Chair 1

A rocking chair presents a fascinating problem in design, and there are really two types. The first could be described as a dining chair with arms and set on to slightly curved rocker rails (28″–30″) with about a $1\frac{1}{2}$″–2″ rise at both ends. The other type as shown could be described as a high back easy chair with a fuller movement set on rockers (36″), with a 4″ rise at both ends. The curve of the rocker is an arc of a circle. The height of the arm can be 21″ and the side frame members $1\frac{1}{4}$″ thick by 2″ at the top corners but increasing to $2\frac{1}{2}$″ wide at the bottom corners and the rocker rail is 2″ wide at floor level. Comb joints are used at the corners although mortise and tenon joints could be used. It will be noticed that the shoulders on the side rails are square and if tapered blocks are glued on at appropriate points the gluing will be made easier. A diagonal check must be made after gluing.

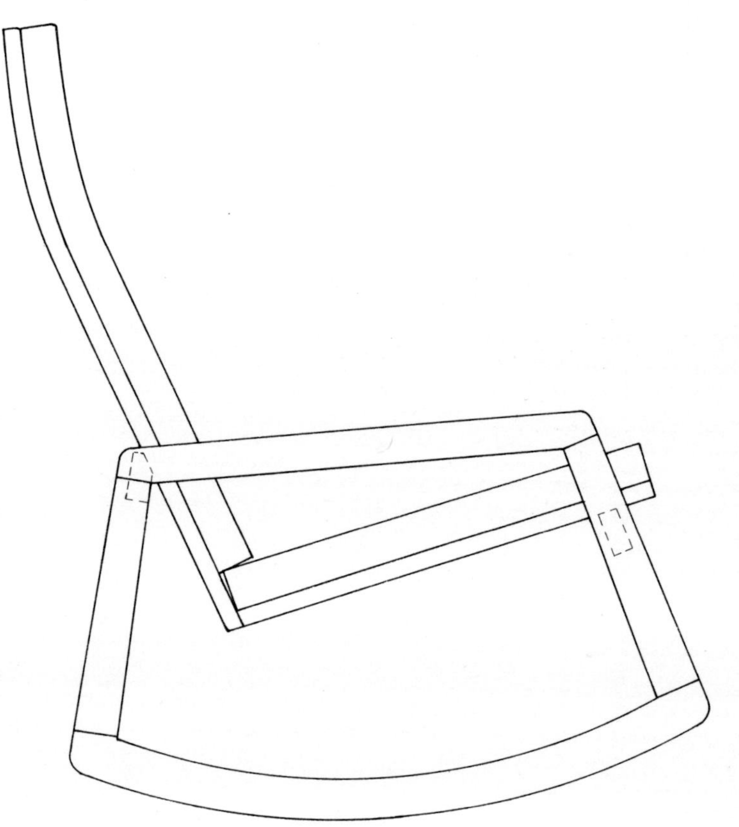

It is now essential to sit down in an easy chair to decide on two very important measurements. How high do you want the back (from the surface of the seat cushion) and also how long do you want the seat (from the surface of the back cushion) ? The rocker shown was made to certain requirements. The back measurement (from surface of seat) is 31″ and the seat (from surface of back) is 22″. The width of the cushions is 20″ and they can be 2″ thick.

The back frame will be 34″ (3″ longer than the foam cushion) but the seat frame will remain at 22″. The back frame looks difficult to make but it is really quite easy. The long rails are made from 2″ wide lengths of ply. These are glued together (total thickness $\frac{3}{4}$″—$\frac{7}{8}$″) and can be nailed along the straight piece to prevent slip, but no nails must be in the area of the corner joint. They are then clamped together on to the simple former.

Bridle joints on side frames.

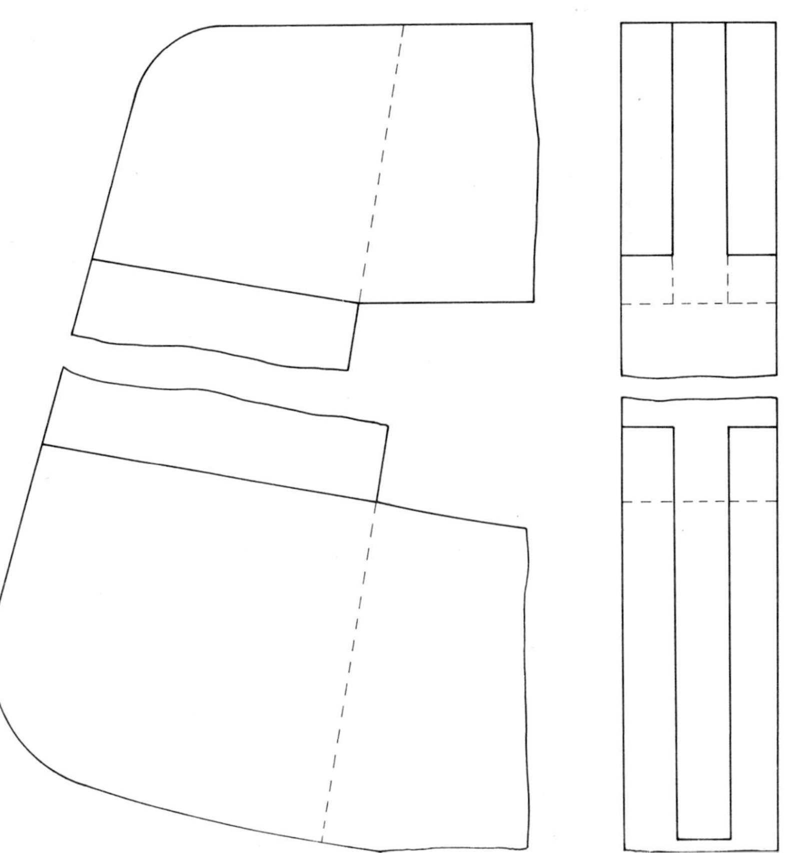

c

These rails and all others, which should be cut from
2" wide batten, can be comb jointed or mortised
and tenoned at the corners. 2" rubber webbing is
nailed across the back and one length nailed
vertically. 2" rubber webbing has been used for
the back to prevent excessive sagging which would
distort the back cover of the chair. Rubber webbing
should run from front to back on the seat frame and
the rubber should be stretched $\frac{1}{2}$" for every 10" of
span.

1 Alternative joints for cross rails.

2 Back frame joints. Webbing tacked on and back
  material in place for wrapping round.

3 Material wrapped round and tacked down.

4 Flap sewn into rear of back cushion cover.

5 Flap of back cushion cover tacked on to back
  frame.

6 Finished back with cushion in place.

The angle between the back and seat frames is usually about 100°, but if you would like to experiment with this then the two frames can be joined with a strip of tin plate at the meeting edges to form a flexible joint. This strip will form a permanent joint and in some ways is better than screwing.
Now having made the two side frames and having the 2″ foam in place, the frames should be set with four G cramps into a rocking position and tried by the person who is going to use the chair. When a final position is decided then cross rails (2″ × 1″) can be dowelled or mortised and tenoned into position. The frames can be screwed through onto the rails when the back is covered with material. FINISH : Paint or clear lacquer.

Blocks glued on before gluing frame.

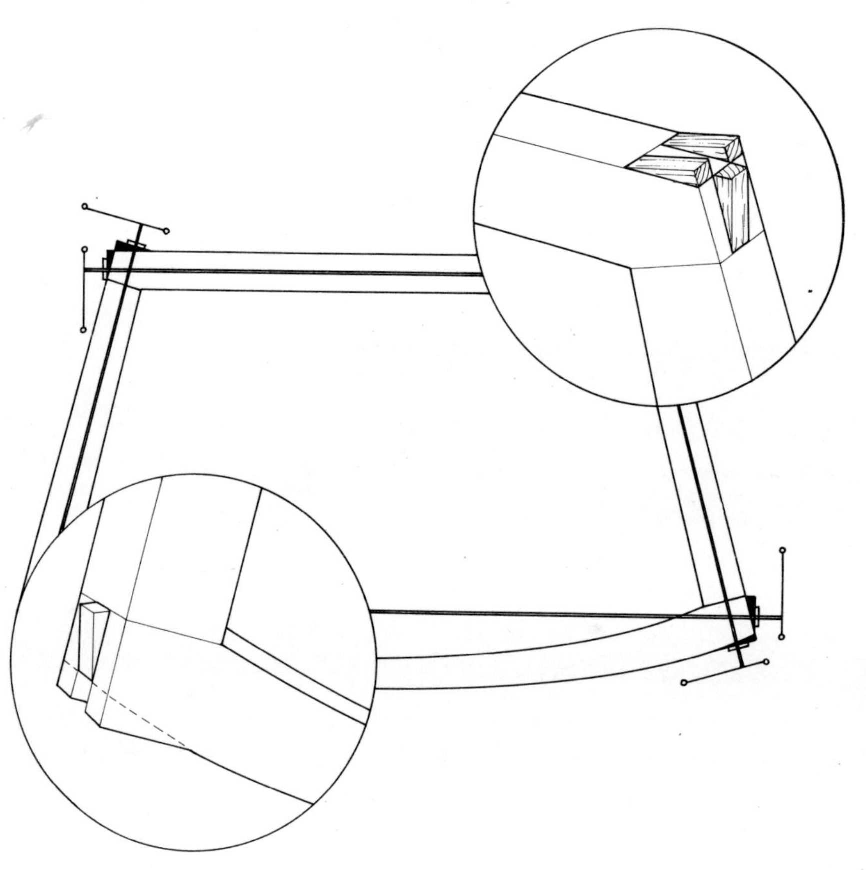

7   Underside of frames joined together to show
    flexible tin plate joint for free testing of seat
    position in frame.

8   Jig for forming back rails.

9   Ply strips in jig.

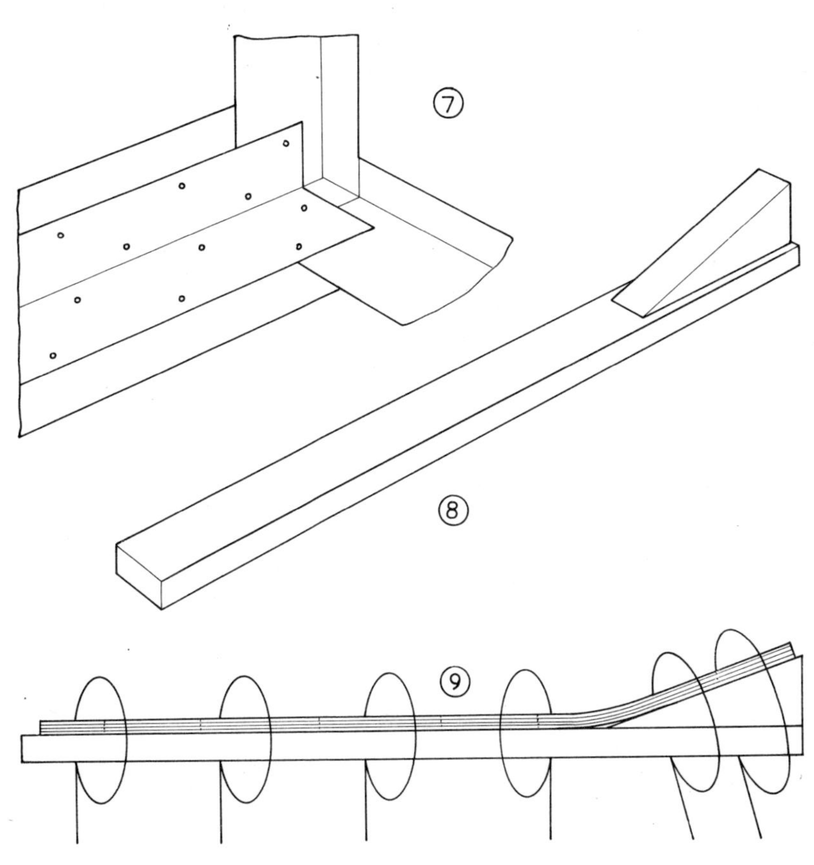

Rocking Chair 2

This chair is made mainly from $\frac{5}{8}$" blockboard or plywood, $\frac{1}{4}$" plywood and 2" × $\frac{3}{4}$" batten. The sides of $\frac{5}{8}$" blockboard or plywood can be finished with a white acrylic emulsion paint and the cushions upholstered in a brightly coloured material. The sides are about 36" long by 22" deep—including the armrest and rocker rail. The armrest is about 26" long. The inside width is 20", the seat cushion 19" × 20" and the back cushion 20" × 32". It is a good plan to draw a full size side elevation of the chair.

The sides can also be made from two layers of $\frac{3}{8}$" ply with the centre of one cut out to give a panelled effect. This could be used for a colour treatment. Again, $\frac{1}{2}$" blockboard and $\frac{3}{16}$" ply would form an effective combination for a panelled treatment when glued together.

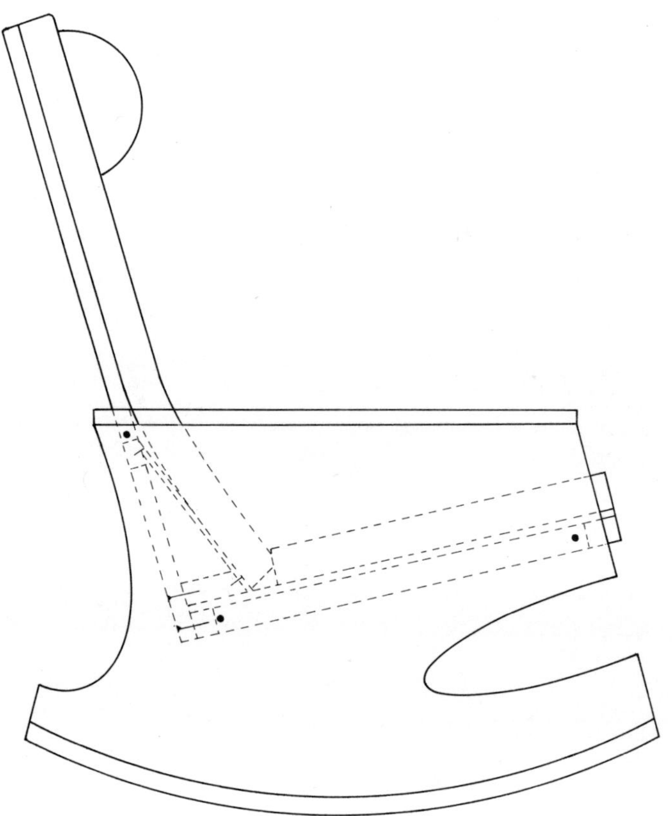

The sides can be left without the curved cut-outs shown,.in which case straight $\frac{3}{8}$" lippings can be glued directly on to the front and back edges using Resin W adhesive. If the sides are cut away (as in sketch) then a thin $\frac{1}{8}$" lipping will be sufficiently flexible to bend to the curves.

1 Arm rest and lower rail dowelled on to side frame. Lower rail can be screwed.

2 Edges of cut-away blockboard being lipped, using string round nails on battens clamped to side frames. Lipping can also be fixed using veneer pins. These can be punched in or withdrawn and holes filled.

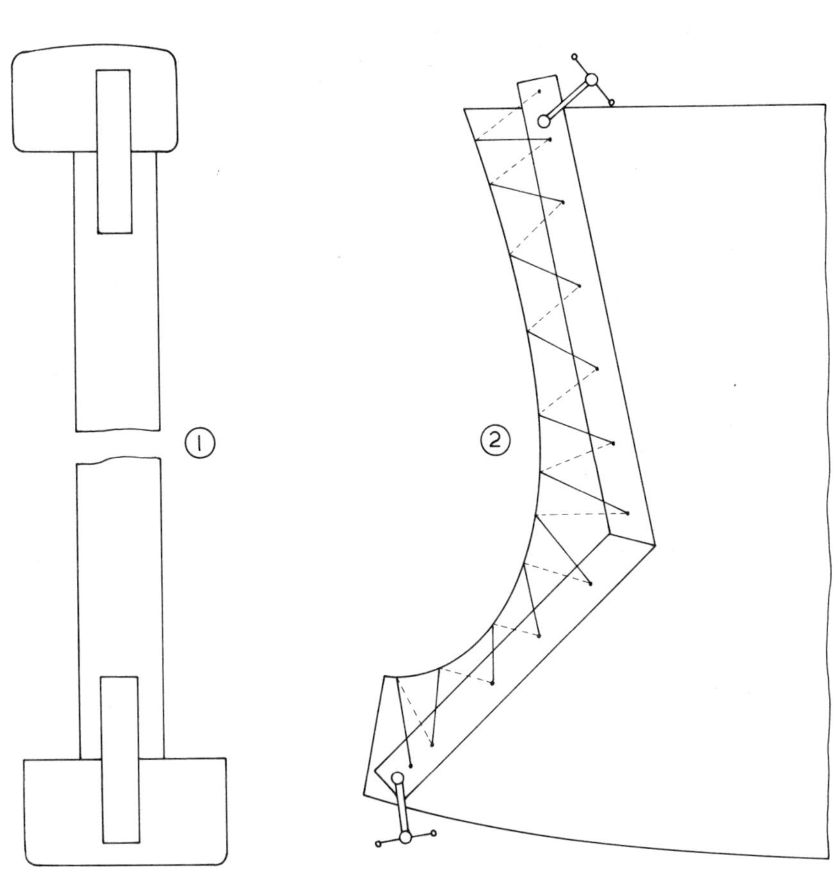

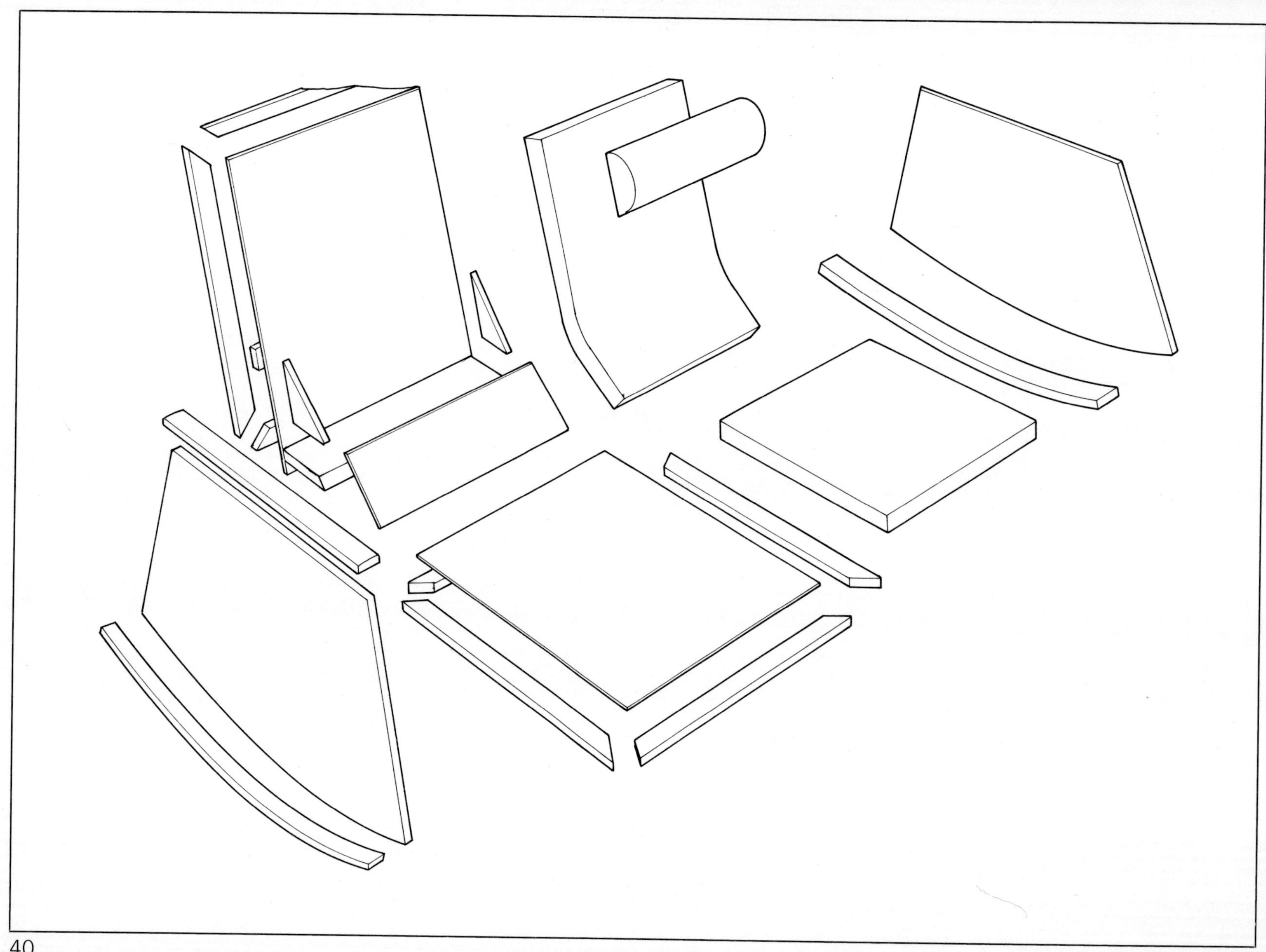

Once again if Resin W is used then the lippings can be glued directly onto the blockboard but if $\frac{5}{8}$" ply is used lipping will be unnecessary.
The bottom rail is made from four pieces of $1\frac{1}{2}$" × $\frac{3}{16}$" material glued together using the side as a former. The arm rest can be made from $1\frac{1}{2}$" × $\frac{3}{4}$" material.
The seat and back are made from $\frac{1}{4}$" ply with a glued and pinned edging of 2" × $\frac{3}{4}$" material. The seat and back frames are then glued and screwed together (95°−100°) and a $\frac{3}{16}$" ply lumber support is also glued and nailed into position.

3 Using side as a former.

4 Panels can be made by gluing two sheets together.

5, 6, 7 Other treatments. Circles laid on or cut out.

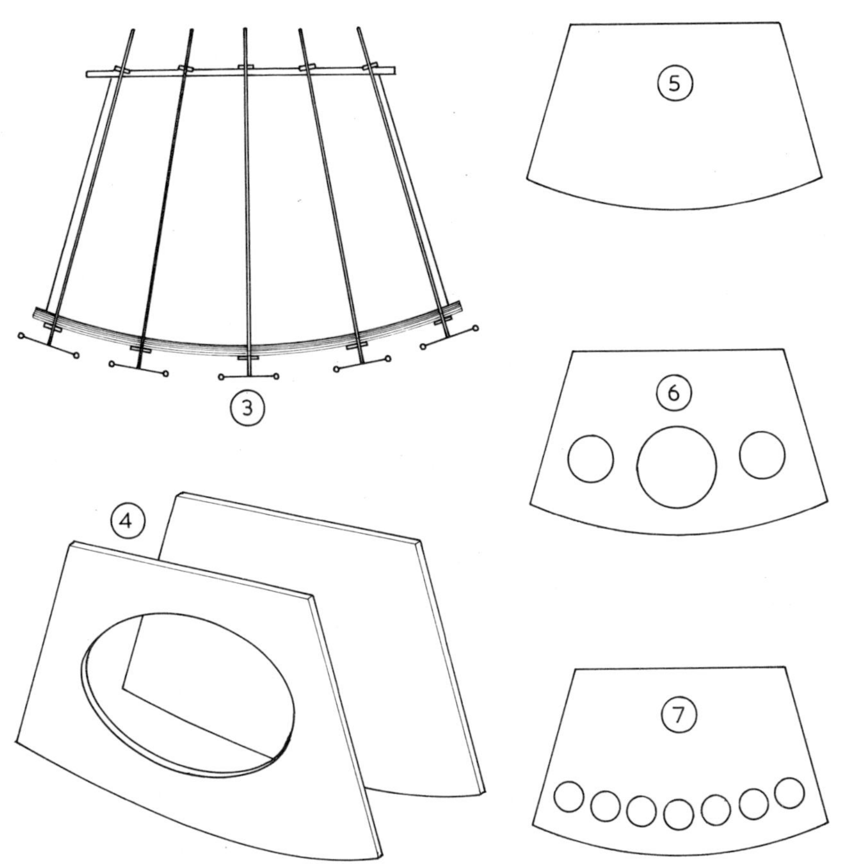

The seat and back can also be made as shown in Rocking Chair No. 1 or made from sheets of $\frac{5}{8}''$ blockboard or ply.

The seat-back may now be cramped to the sides for testing the rocking movement. The foam should be in position for testing as this will affect the balance. Thoroughly test the chair at this stage before finally bolting together. This is also the best stage at which to consider the cut out shapes (as in sketch) as these relate to the seat and back positions.

When the best position is found and marked the $\frac{1}{4}''$ holes should be drilled through the sides and frames for the $3'' \times \frac{1}{4}''$ dia. countersunk metal screws.

Back cushion cover showing :

 8 Boxed corners.

 9 Back panel.

10 Press stud flap at lumbar support.

11 Zip fastener if required.

12 Open seam for entry of nailing-down flap.

13 Nailing-down flap sewn from inside.

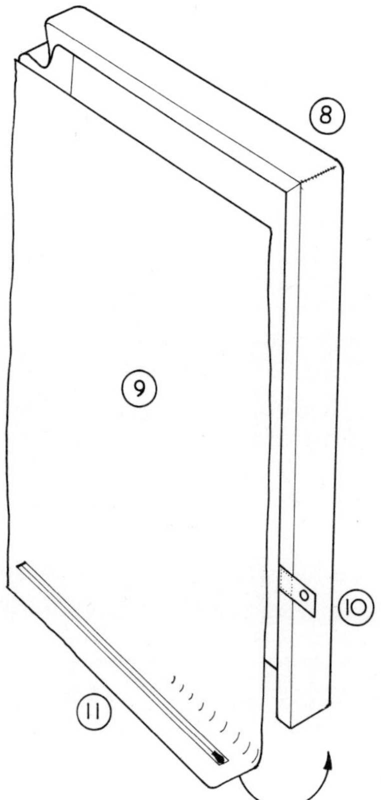

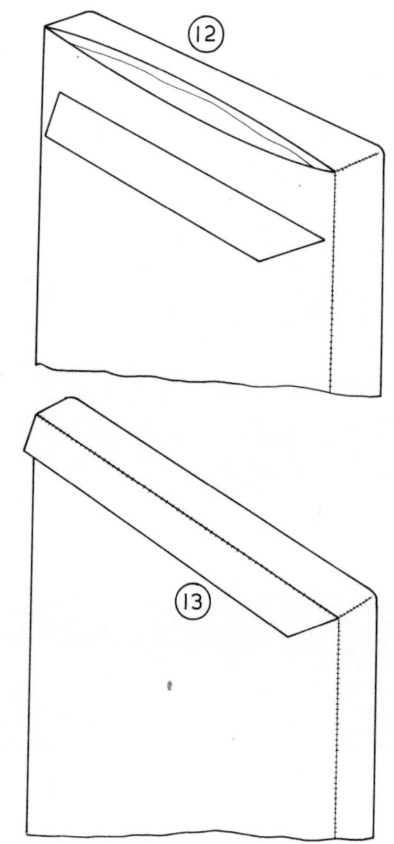

As the back is covered with material before it is fixed between the sides, access for bolting is blocked and a tapped strip of steel $2'' \times \frac{3}{4}'' \times \frac{1}{4}''$ can be screwed on to the inside of the back frame into which the screw or bolt may be secured.

14, Pillow covers made by ends—6″ diameter
15, semi-circles sewn in. Back seam left open in
16 middle for lining filled with feathers, crumbled foam or formed foam.

17 Sections through strap.

18 Press-fasteners in place.

19 Material tacked on back (front view).

20 Pillow adjusting straps tacked to back before cushion flap is nailed into position (front view).

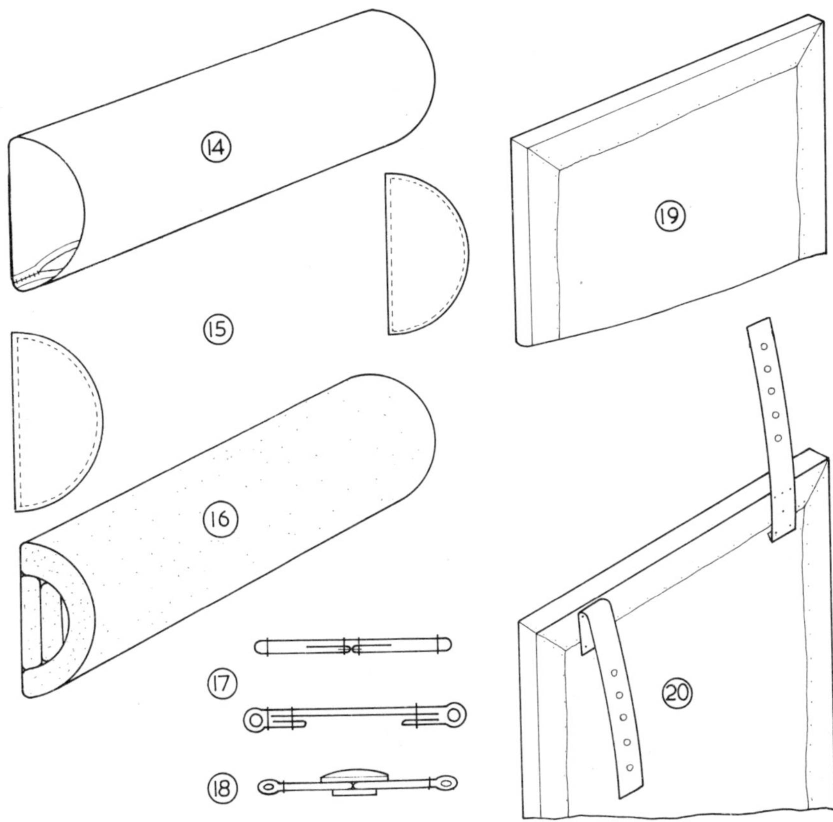

21 Pillow straps hanging over back cushion.

22 Neck pillow in place.

23 Alternative way of fixing ply frame to seat—by gluing onto side.

24 Alternative way of fixing blockboard seat to side—by gluing and screwing rail to side and then screwing down seat.

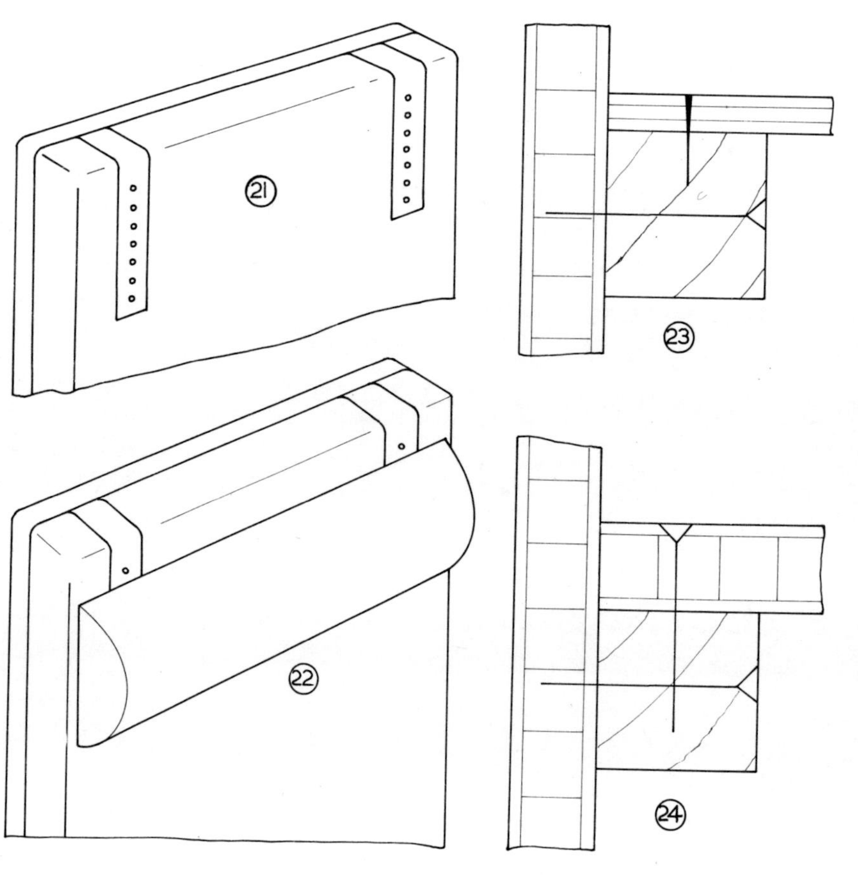

25 Bracket let in and screwed to arm.

26 Chair back in position screwed to bracket.

27 Tapped plate screwed on to back rail. Back rail screwed to side frame.

28 Seat frame bolted through side frame. This method can also be used on the back if a hole is cut through the ply to give access to nut (back will be covered with fabric).

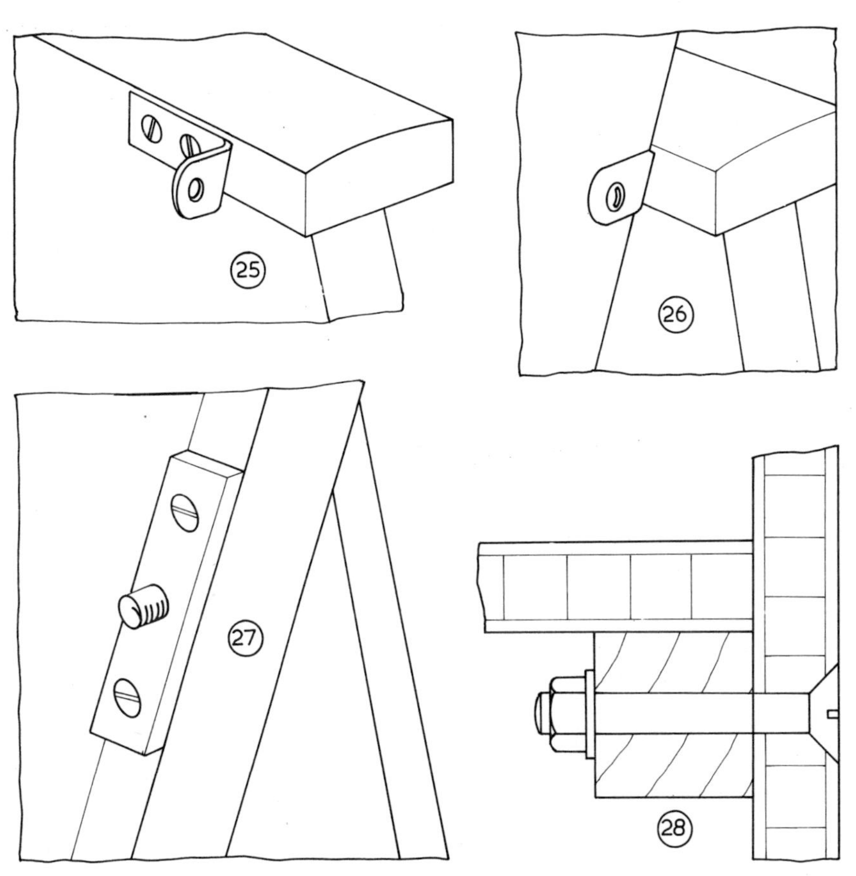

Round Coffee Table

The table has three legs and three laminated rails which are formed from plywood. A $\frac{1}{2}$" thick rail would be suitable for a 24" dia. and $\frac{5}{8}$" would give extra strength on a 36" dia. top. You must decide on the size and make a plan to determine the curves on the rails. Odd strips of ply can be purchased cheaply or new material cut. An inside former for bending can be made from odd pieces of wood nailed and glued together. Great care must be taken not to get nails too near to an edge which is to be cut.
A rail width of 3" would require a former of approximately that depth. The surface of the former may be waxed to prevent the ply from gluing to it. The number of strips will depend on the thickness of ply being used.

They should be glued and cramped on to the former
and an extra two strips will help to distribute the
pressure and prevent the cramps from damaging
the surface of the rail. The rails can be cleaned to
width and glued together. Some little shaping may
be required on the inner gluing faces.
If teak legs are being used then a teak veneer can
be laid on to the rails when being formed, in which
case a double layer of paper should be placed
between the veneer and the outer layers of plywood
which are protecting the veneered surface.

1   Former blocks cut for gluing and nailing.

2   Former cut and shaped.

3   Ply for rail and two protective strips to protect
    and distribute pressure.

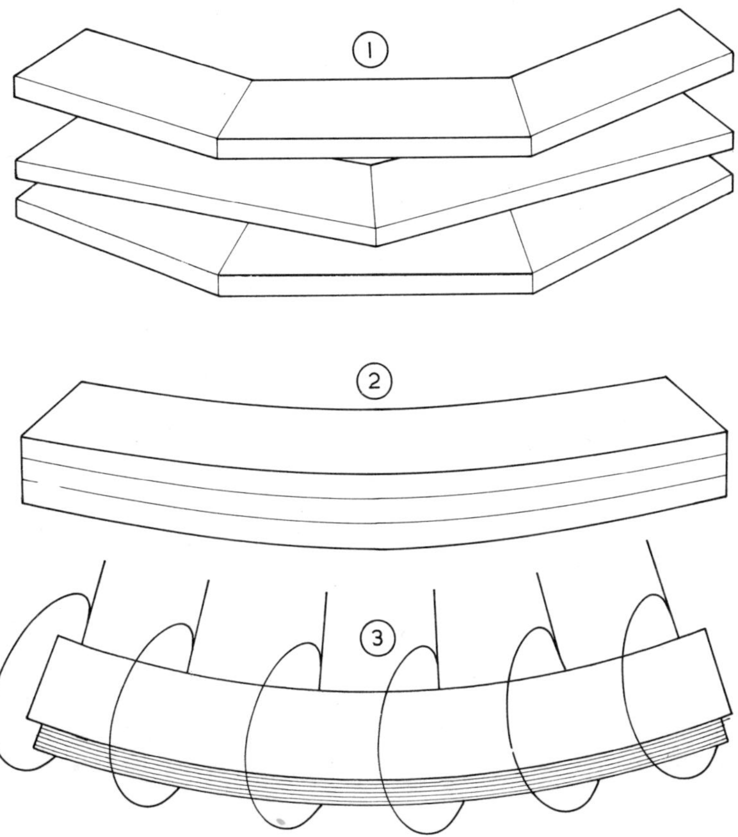

The horns at the top of the legs can be cut off before
gluing the legs onto the frame. This will avoid
difficult cleaning at a later stage. The joints can be
glued by placing a fairly thick batten opposite and
cramping from that . Legs can be glued on
separately ; their edges can be well rounded.
The top is made from $\frac{5}{8}$" blockboard and can be
finished in a number of ways. In any case a $\frac{1}{8}$" thick
lipping is desirable. If this is cut slightly wider than
the thickness of the blockboard not much cleaning
up will be required after it is glued on. It may be
glued on in one, two, three or even more lengths.
Battens with nails protruding are clamped to both
surfaces and the lipping is secured with strong
string. The ends are long—scarfed after the glue
is set and the next length is laid on top without
scarfing and trimmed into the circle when it is set.
This method will make a good join, especially if a
sash cramp is placed across the table top where the
joint is being made.

4 Tenon cut into rails formed from plywood.

5 Plates for fixing top to frame.

6 Arrangement of dowels as alternative joints.

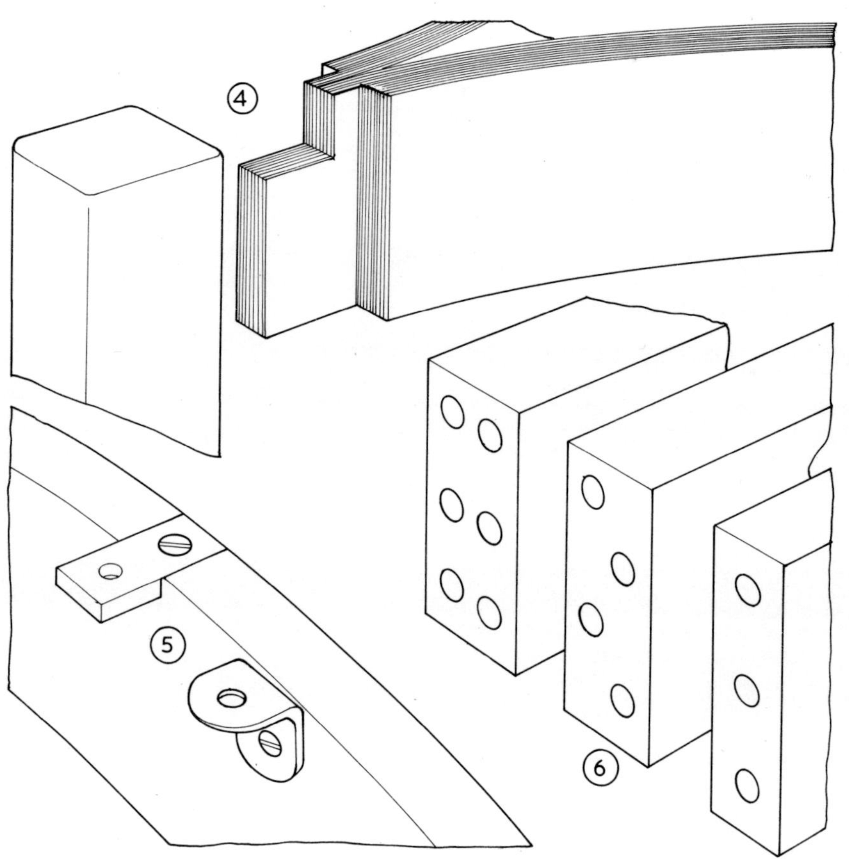

7 Cramping leg to frame using shaped blocks on
   the rail.

8 Sash cramp on scarf joint.

9 Gluing lipping to edge of table top. Sellotape or
   gummed strip can also be used for veneer strips.

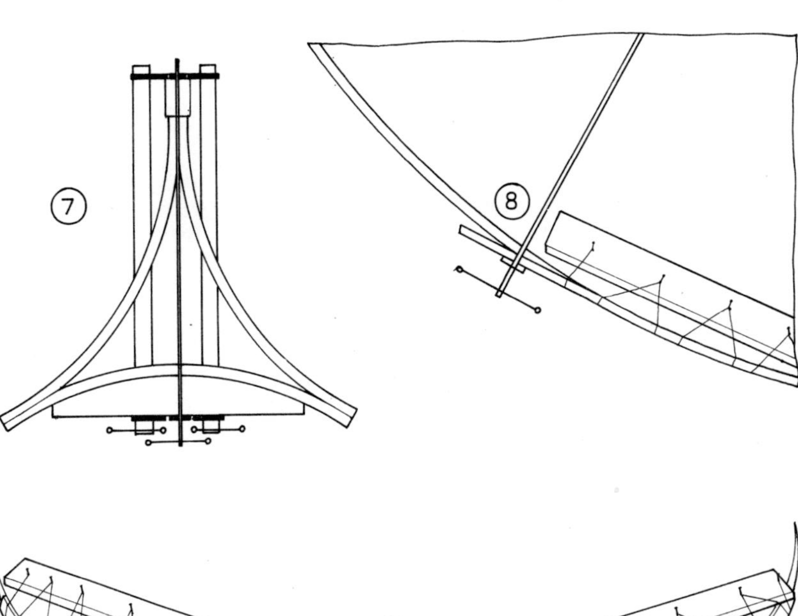

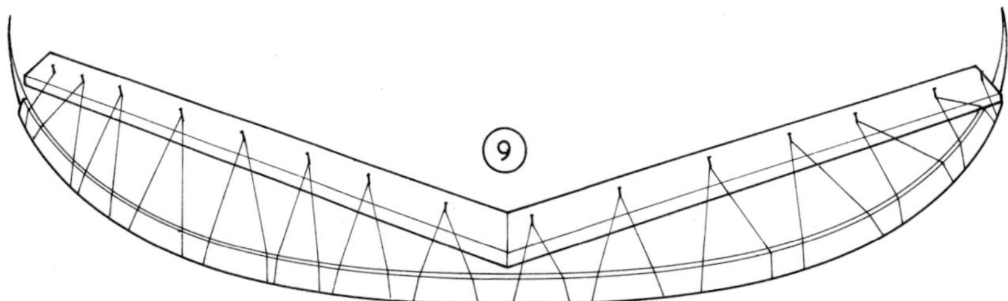

The surface can now be filled and painted with sanding sealer or polyurethane or acrylic emulsion paint. These paints are tough and durable. A good surface can be produced by filling with sanding sealer or Polyfilla or a similar cellulose filler. Two or three coats of paint may now be applied. When the paint is dry it can be rubbed down with 320 grade silicon carbide wet or dry paper. When used with water a fine smooth surface can be obtained before a final coat of paint is applied using brush or spray.

Alternatively the surface may be veneered if a press is available. Again the surface can be finished with plastic laminate. If a press is not available the edges should be lipped as described and a contact glue used for the laminate. If the top is laid flat on the floor and well "danced on" (without shoes !) a good contact can be made. The edges are effectively secured by the use of a small engineer's vice (protected jaws) or G cramp with extended faces. The blockboard and plastic laminate are now nipped all round. If the pressure is left on for about 10 secs. in each position it will be found that the two will join nicely together.

The surface could be faced with lino. The surface should be well glued with Resin W and the lino pressed on by using another sheet of blockboard and weighting down. The edges are now trimmed and the lipping applied. Considerable care must be taken not to damage the surface of the lino when gluing on the lipping and also when cleaning it down.

The top and underframe can be joined together using flat plates or angle plates. Both can be made from suitable strip, but angle plates can also be bought.

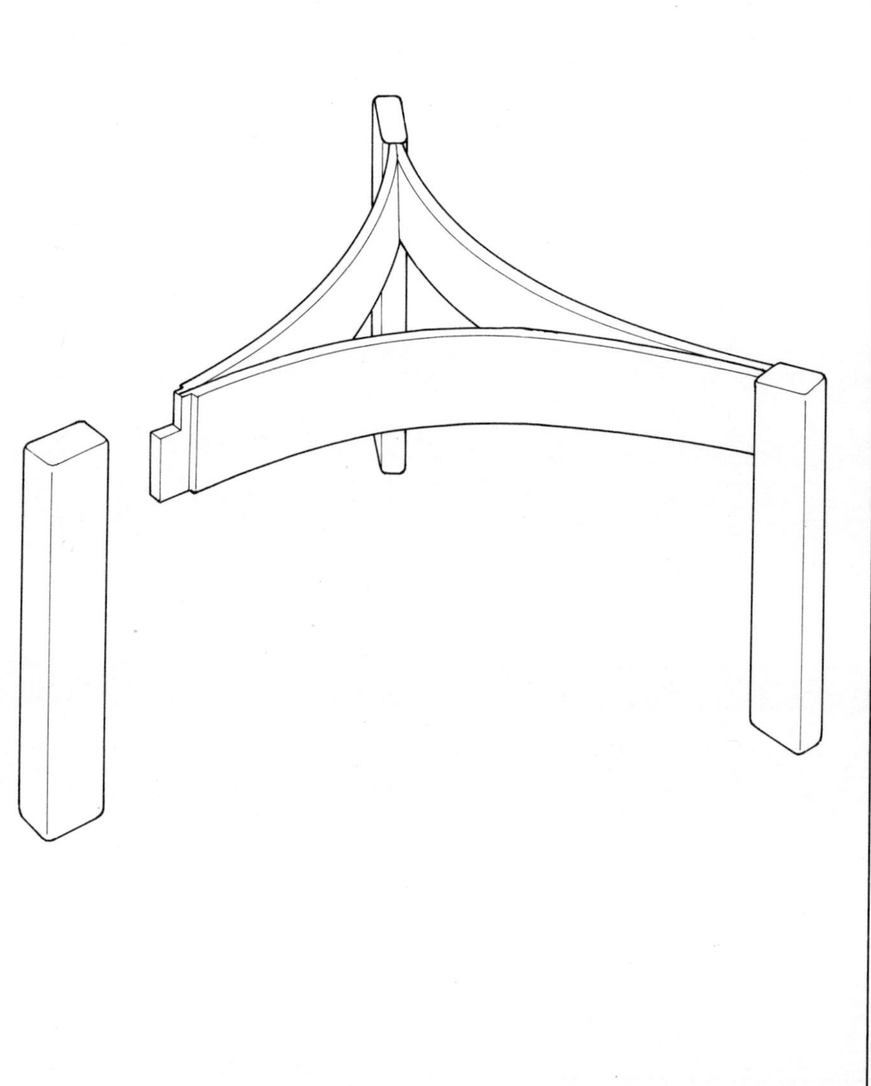

Book Storage Unit

This useful free-standing unit combines the functions of coffee table, seat and storage for magazines and books. It is made quite simply from ½″ blockboard which can be painted or veneered. The top can also be covered in plastic laminate or lino.

The width is 16″ but could be more or less, depending on the size of books to be stored. By moving the centre stop rail larger books can be stored on one side than on the other. The depth of the book storage is 10″ and once again this can be adjusted as required. The drawer-magazine compartment is 3″ or 4″ deep and the overall height can be 16″—18″. The length can be as required and this measurement will be conditioned to some extent by how much the unit is to be moved about. Closing strips are placed under the bottom shelf to keep dust from under the unit. The blockboard is lipped with ⅜″ material and this can be glued on directly to the edges if Resin W adhesive is used. A very sharp, finely set plane should be used for planing the lipping down to the blockboard surface, which should not be disturbed in this operation.

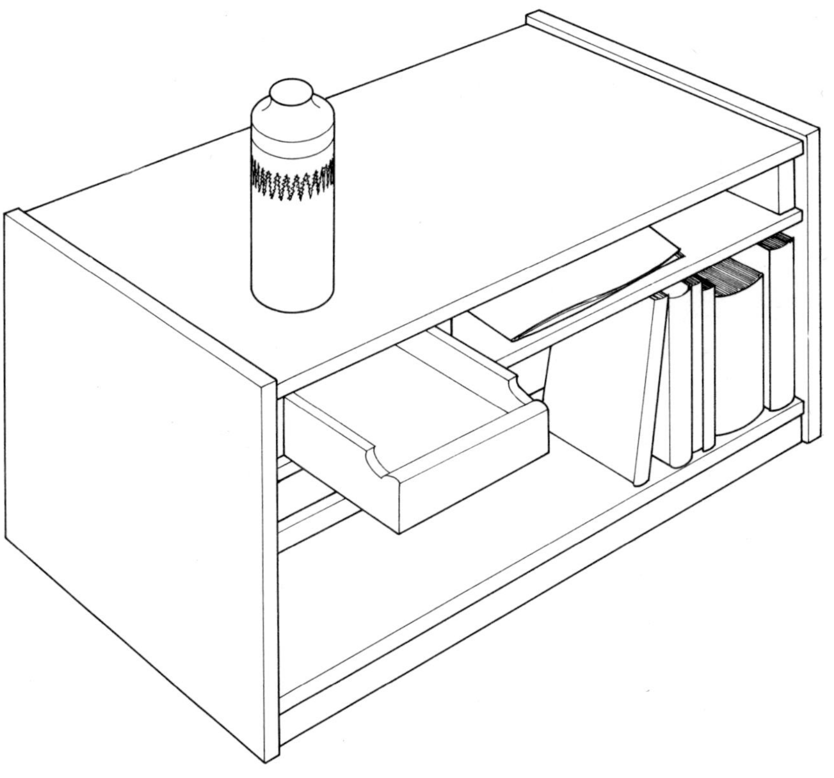

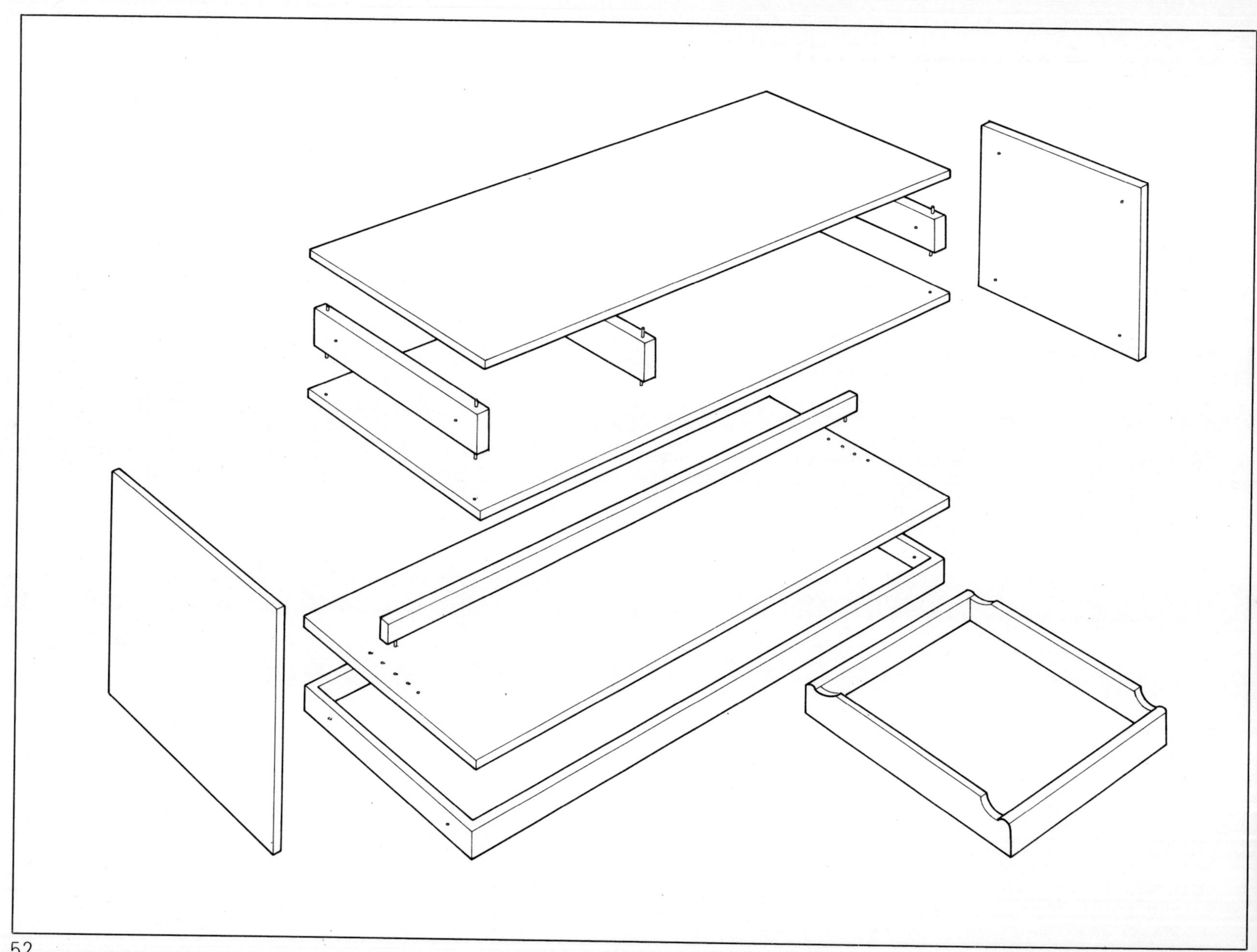

Basically the structure consists of two boxed up frames—upper for the drawer and magazine compartment and a lower for the book shelf. These are made to have considerable areas at the ends to which the end panels can be glued, bolted or screwed. The three spacing rails in the drawer-magazine compartment can be about $\frac{7}{8}$" thick and $\frac{1}{4}$" locating dowels are fitted to make the gluing easier.

Top and bottom: Various forms of unit.

1 Assembly.

Methods of assembly:

2 Screwing with head in cup.

3 Coach bolt with polished and lacquered or painted head.

4 Countersunk head.

5 Screwing from inside.

6 Dowel for location before gluing.

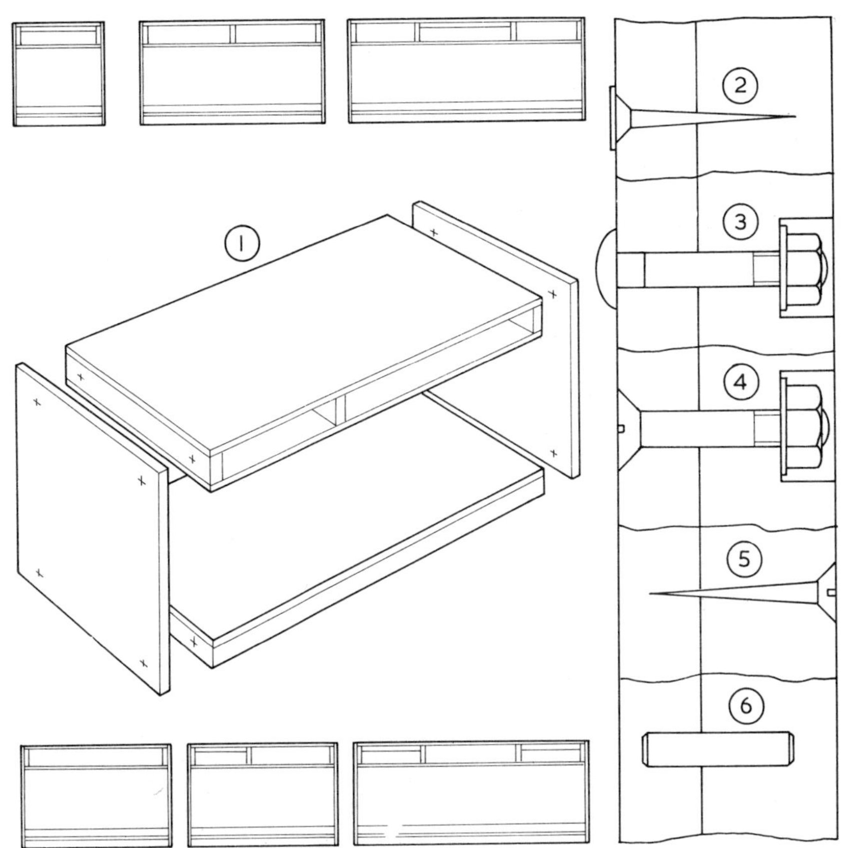

The book adjusting bar can be set on dowels with about five positions. The underframe can be dowelled or dovetailed and the bookshelf can be glued to the frame. Some location on dowels or pins should be provided. The panel pins should be hammered into the lower frame and then cut off with about $\frac{1}{8}''$ protruding. One at each corner would prevent slip when gluing.

7 Adjusting bar for book widths.

8 Blockboard shelf.

9 Underframe with dowelled joint. Nails protruding for shelf location.

10 Under frame with lap dovetail joint.

11 Top corner of unit showing drawer front.

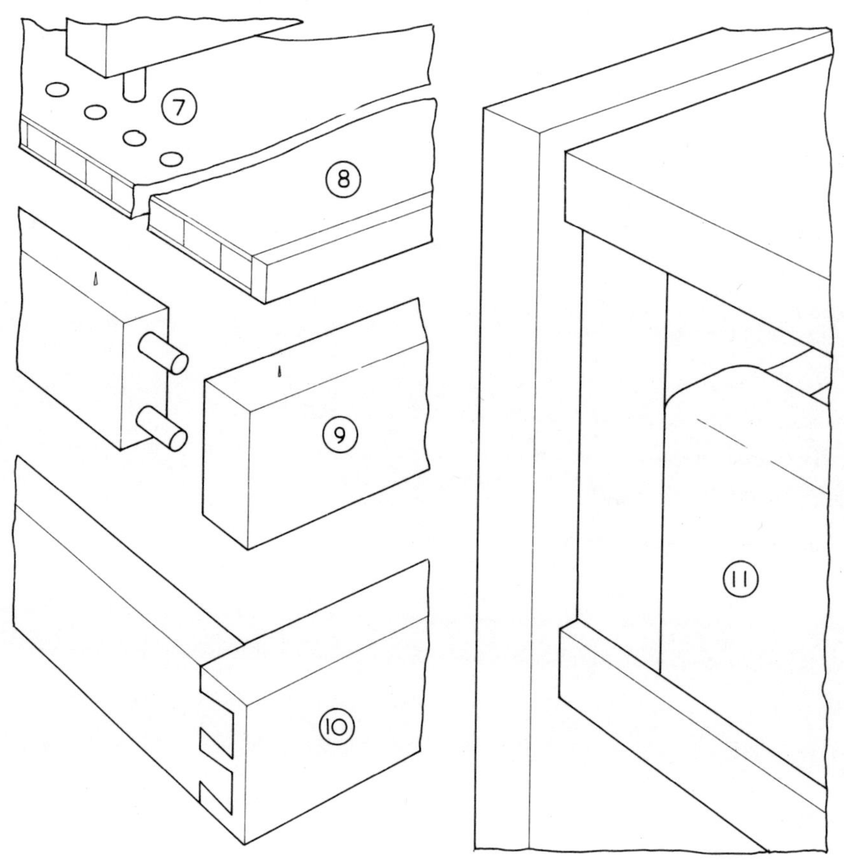

The drawer can be made from $\frac{5}{8}$" material for the ends and $\frac{7}{16}$" for the sides. As the grooves are cut directly into the sides and ends the ply bottom must be entered when gluing. The ends are made so that a hand can enter for opening. The drawer and ply should be fully cleaned and finished before gluing. The ply must not be very tight as a little movement is desirable for diagonal testing and adjustment when gluing.

12 Front elevation of top corner.

13 Side elevation of drawer.

14 Insider corner of drawer.

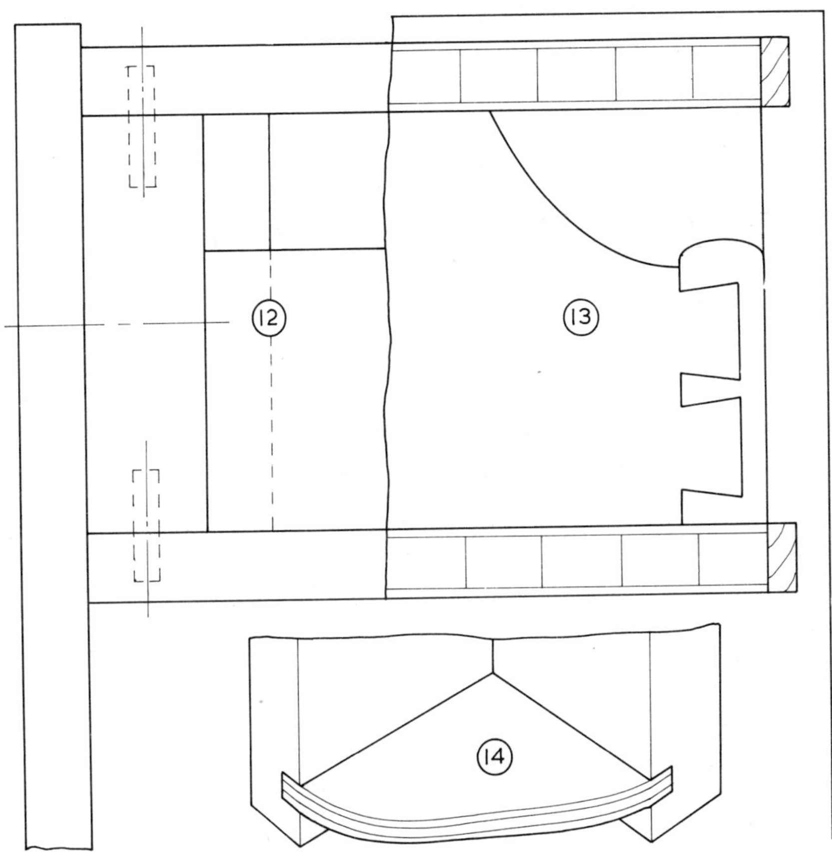

Tea Trolley

The two surfaces on this trolley should be covered with plastic laminate, which is easy to clean and durable. If the end frames are made in teak and finished with teak oil, then a white or black laminate would look pleasing, but many other attractive colours would look well with teak. The height of the top surface above floor level can be 28″ and this should include the castors. The end frames project about 1″ higher to form handles. The width can be about 18″ and the length 26″–30″. The legs can be made from 1″ × 1⅝″ and rails from ¾″ material. The joints are made flush on the inside to make a continuous surface for joining to the drawer and lower frame sections by glue screws or bolts.

The three main surfaces are made from ½″ blockboard and should be lipped on the side edges with ⅜″ material which can be matching teak if used on the end frames. The drawers can be about 3″ deep and the spacing rails about ⅞″ thick to provide adequate gluing for the application of Resin W adhesive. Location between the gluing surfaces is made by dowels and accuracy of spacing should be ensured by the insertion of lengths of wood during the gluing (back and front). A panel of ½″ blockboard—veneered, painted or covered with plastic laminate—can be set in the back and glued at the same time. If ply is used then vertical grooves must be cut in the end frames and also in the ½″ blockboard, in which case the lipping should be about ¾″ wide on the back edges. The retaining strips on the laminate can be secured with about five dowels or screws.

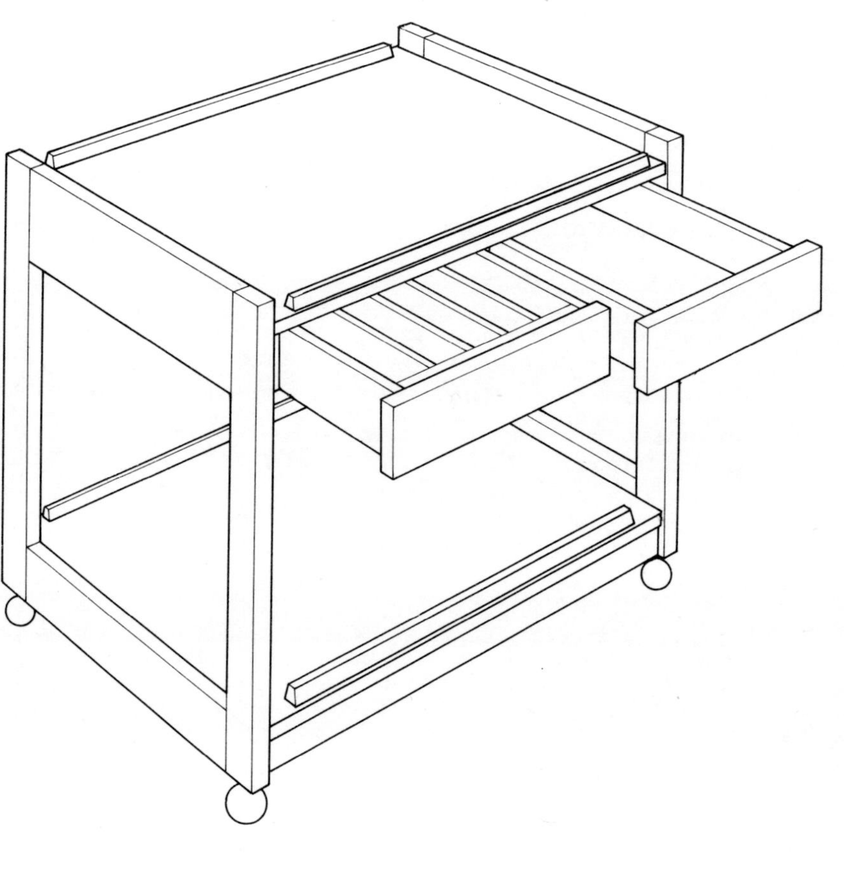

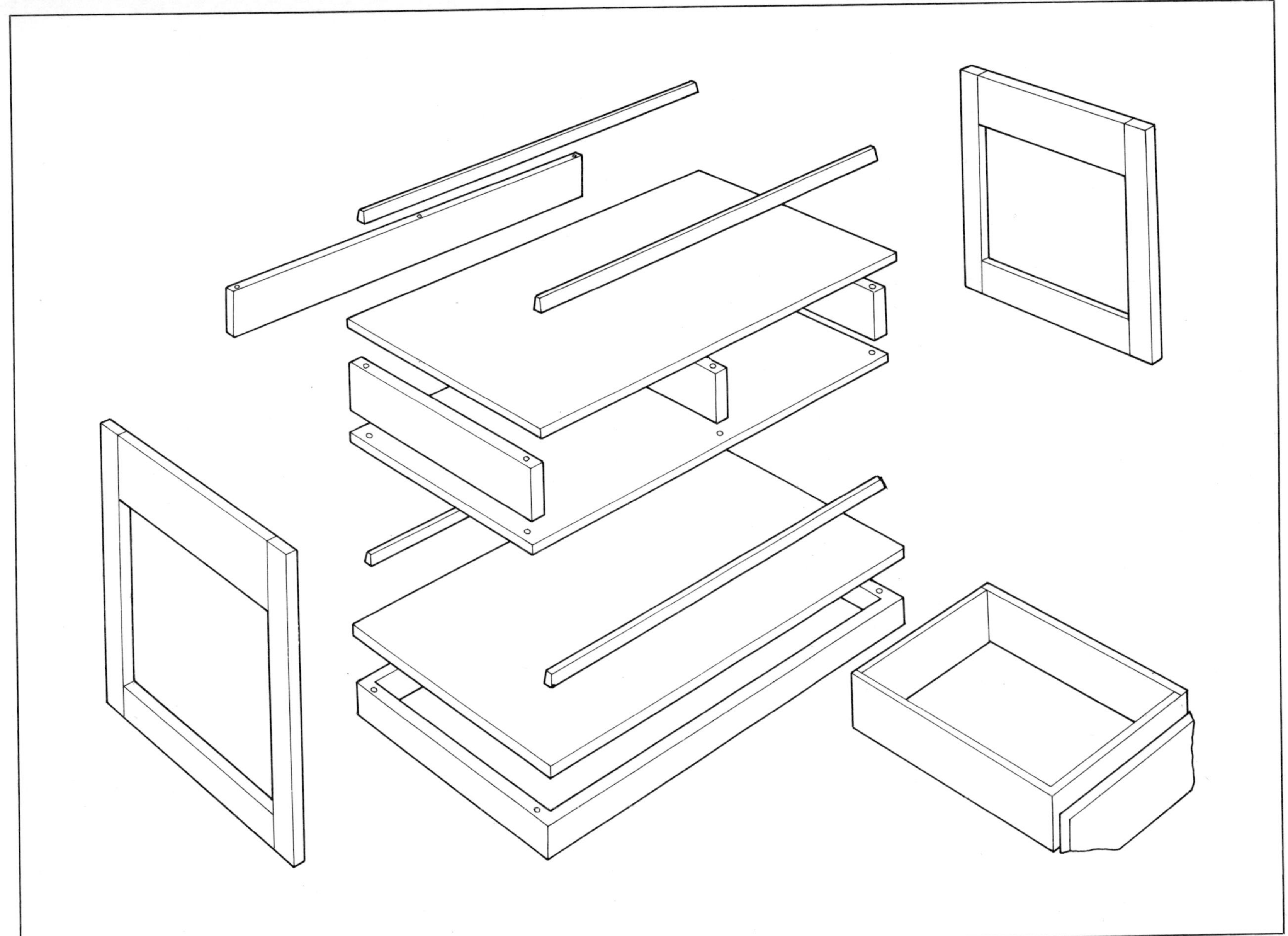

1,2 Mortise and tenon joints in upper and lower rails of end frames.

3,4 Dowel joints in upper and lower rails of end frames (alternative).

5 Lipped lower surface.

6 Lower frame dovetailed at corners.

7 Lower frame dowelled at corners with a glued block (alternative).

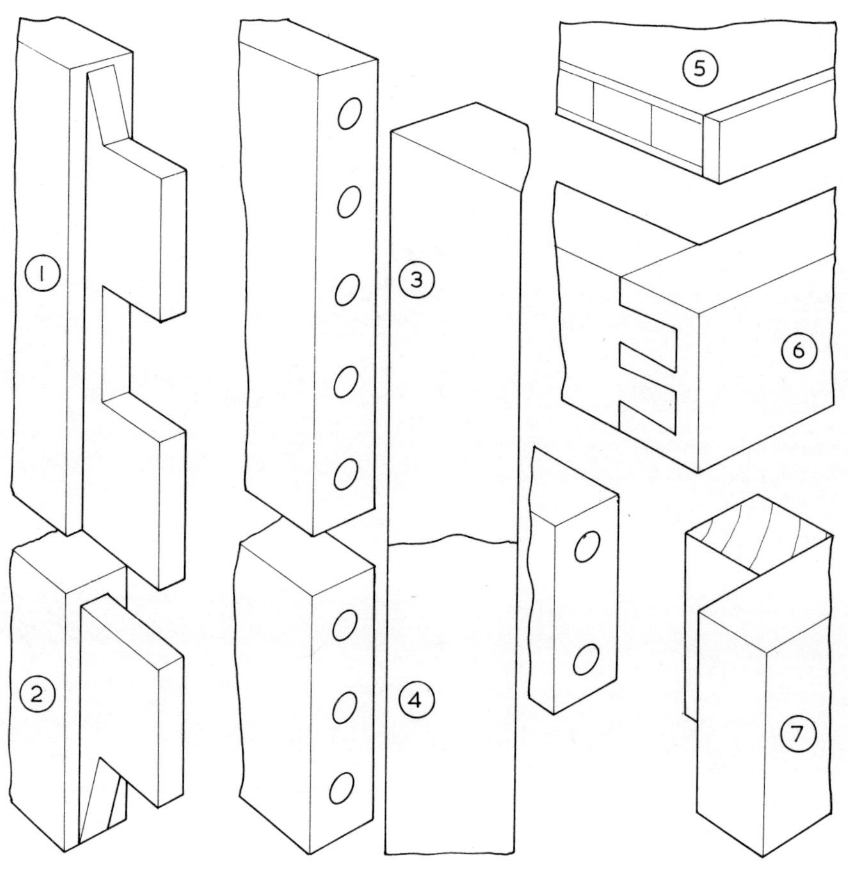

The drawer can be made from $\frac{3}{8}$" material and the fronts laid on by gluing, with two screws from the inside for location.
The laid-on fronts will cover the spacing rails, giving an unbroken surface to the drawer fronts. The laid-on fronts will also project below the blockboard by $\frac{3}{8}$" to provide a handle for the drawer. One drawer can be divided into compartments for cutlery. If a strip of brightly coloured felt or baize is cut to width this may be glued (using Resin W adhesive) into position by starting up one side (A) and continuing along the bottom (B) and over the partition until the covering is complete, when the material can be trimmed with a sharp razor blade against a steel ruler.

8 Section through trolley showing joints on side of drawer.

9 Section through drawer showing ply, partition and run of felt.

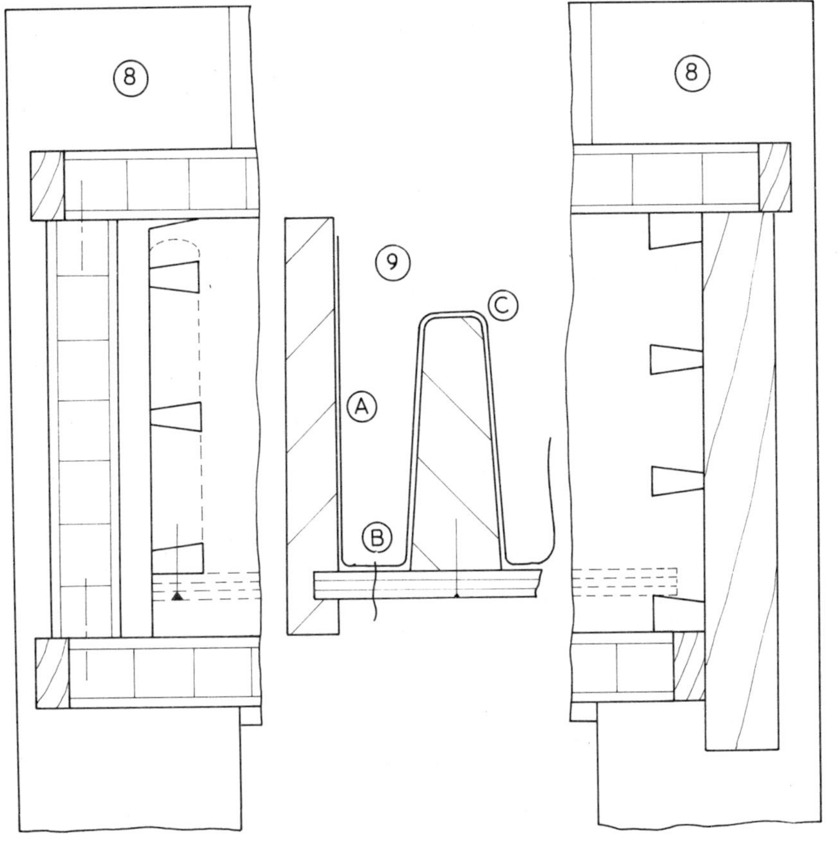

Needlework Trolley 1

This commodious work cabinet incorporates several features giving well ordered storage. The length can be about 22", the height and width between 15"–18". It must be clearly understood that a side elevation should be drawn so that the various features may be seen full size. The lipped blockboard sides are joined together with a $\frac{5}{8}$" bottom, two hinge battens and two partitions providing racks for cottons and wools. The ply base in the well is set on two kicker rails providing continuous running for the two drawers. A half length tray slides on two separate rails. The $\frac{5}{8}$" lipped blockboard ends are hinged and held by nylon cord knotted behind brass plates secured to the falls and the sides of the cabinet. Scissors, wools and needles can be held in pockets— Page 69.

The blockboard can be veneered (if a press is available) or made from veneered blockboard and lacquered. The blockboard can also be painted with hard-wearing polyurethane. The outside of the blockboard can also be completely covered with plastic laminate (technique on page 49) or applied to the top and falls only. An interesting colour scheme can be worked out. A set of small castors can be fitted if required.

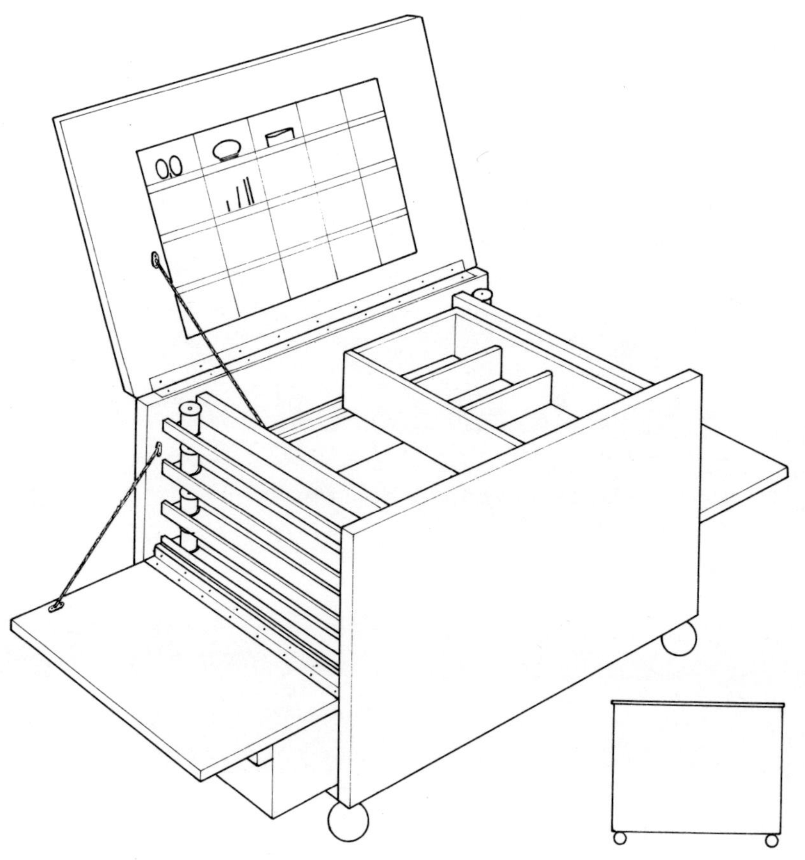

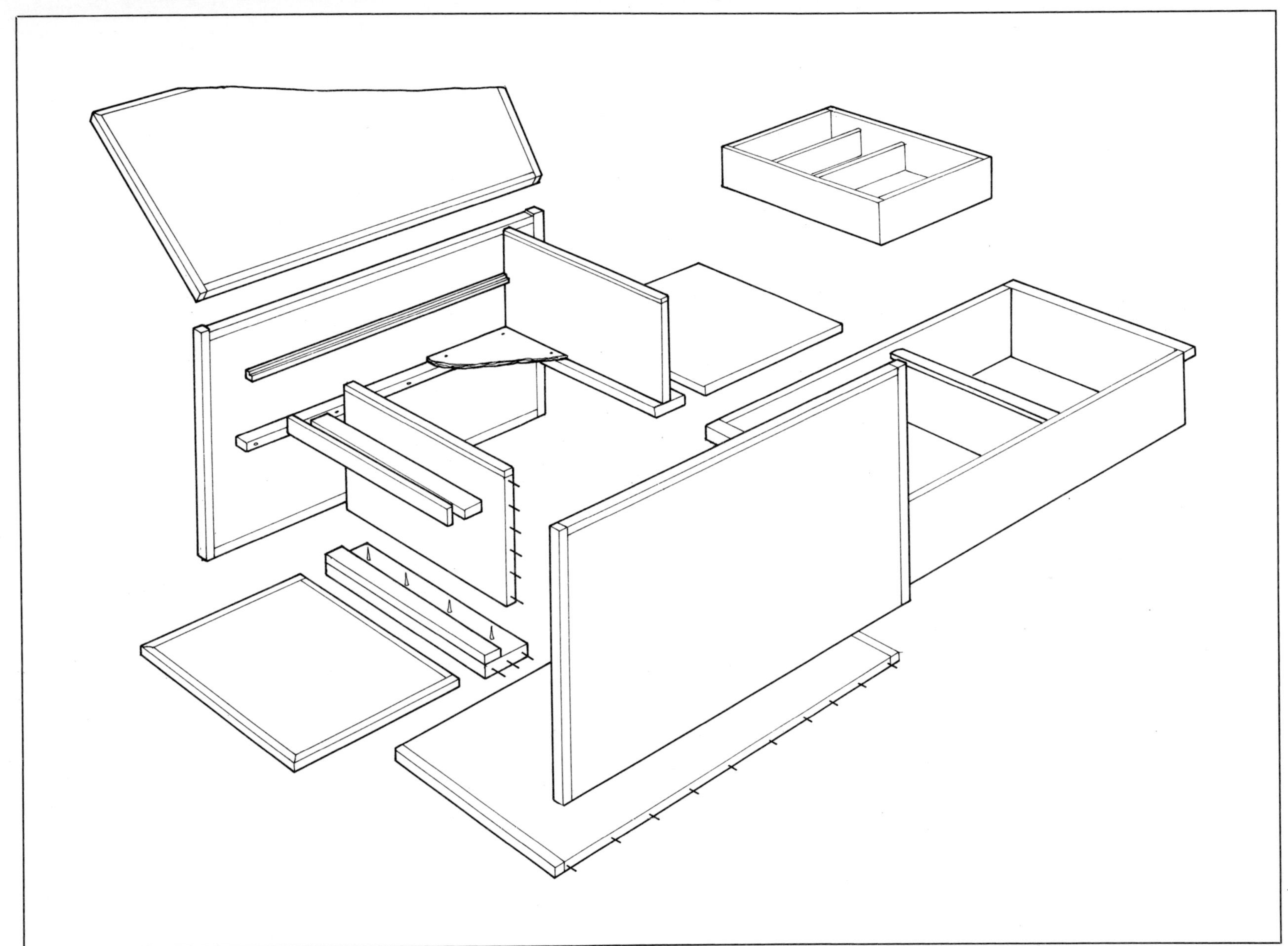

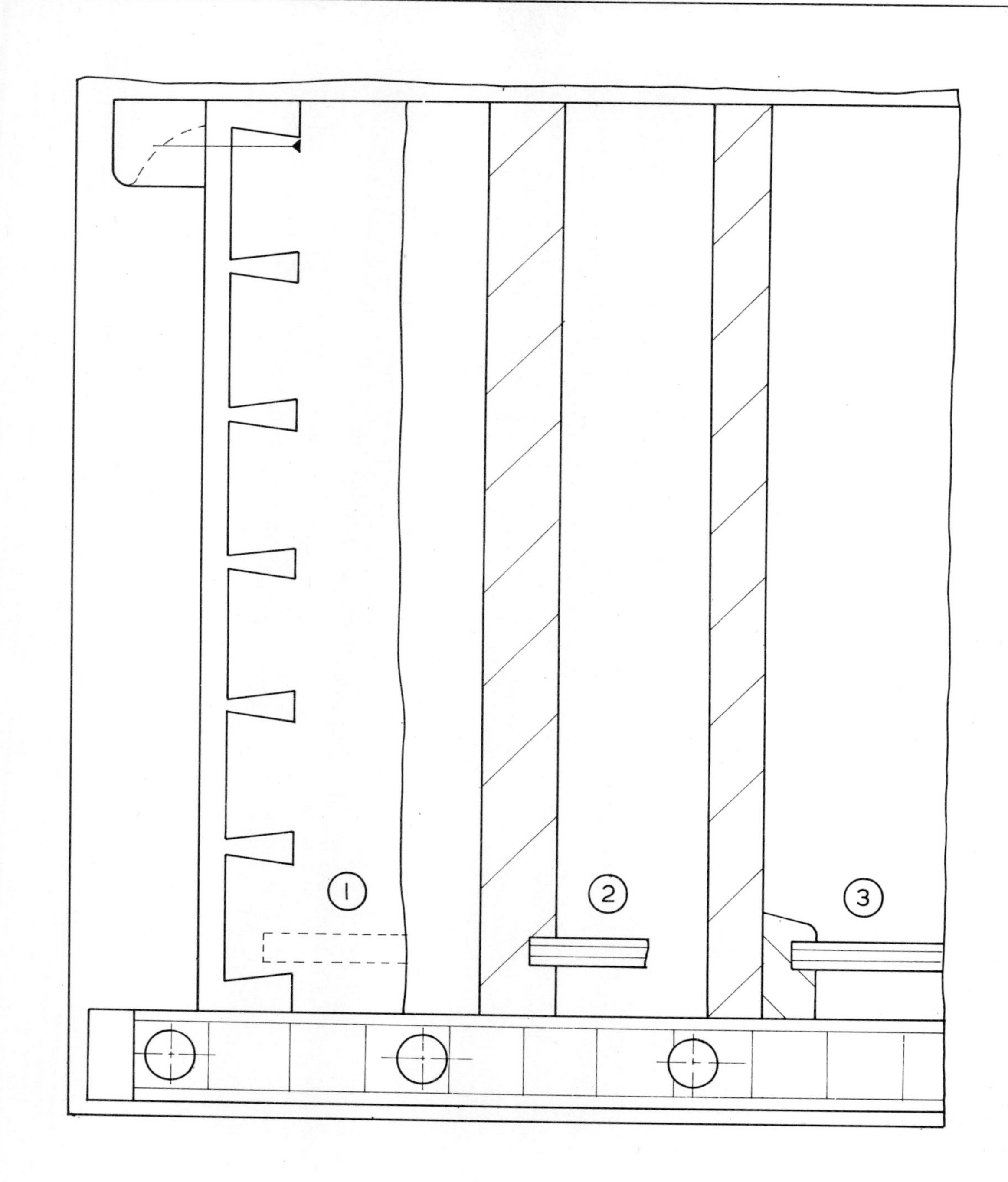

1 Lap dovetails on drawer.

2 Ply let into $\frac{1}{2}$" thick drawer sides.

3 Ply let into slips (glued on to sides before drawer is glued) on $\frac{3}{8}$" drawer sides.

4 Section showing cotton reel racks, end fall, magnetic catch and lid.

5 Section showing tray slide and hinged lid.

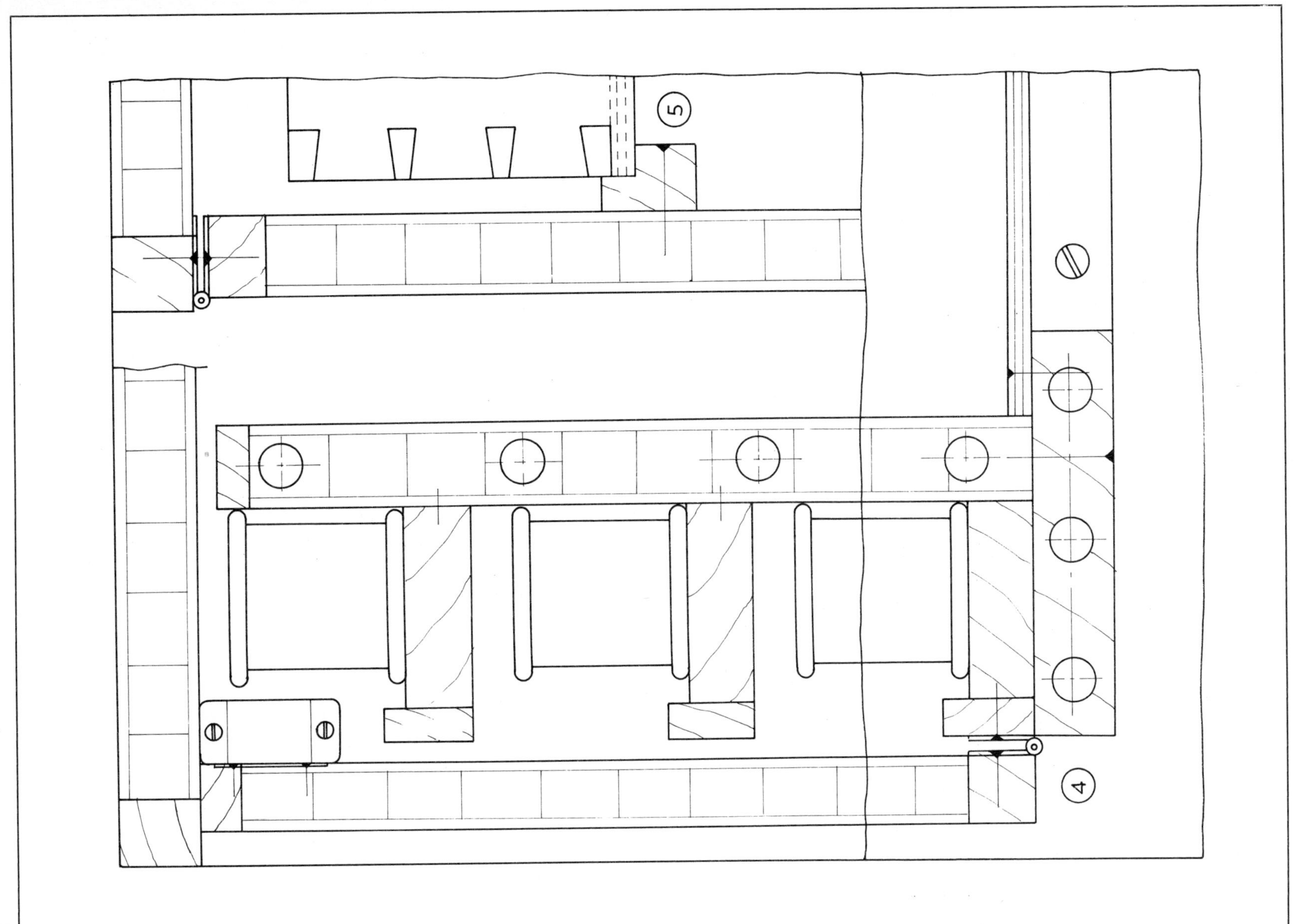

Needlework Trolley 2

This sewing box is made from $\frac{1}{2}$" blockboard and the corners can be made with a simple comb joint and glued, or simply glued and screwed using Resin W as an adhesive. The edges on which the hinge is fitted should be lipped to take the $\frac{1}{2}$" screws. A 1" piano hinge would be suitable but $1\frac{1}{2}$" butt hinges could be used. The bottom is made from $\frac{1}{4}$" or $\frac{3}{16}$" ply and is glued and nailed in. The size of the box must be decided by individual requirements. It could be as small as 18" × 18" × 12" or as large as 24" × 24" × 15". The lid can be veneered, upholstered or covered in plastic laminate to act as a coffee table. The inside sets some interesting problems in storage. A set of small castors will be required.

All edges should be rounded and the outside covered with $\frac{1}{4}$" rubber or plastic carpet underlay (spot glued and tacked). A brightly coloured cloth can now be fitted—Page 68.

Right—Alternative forms of joints.

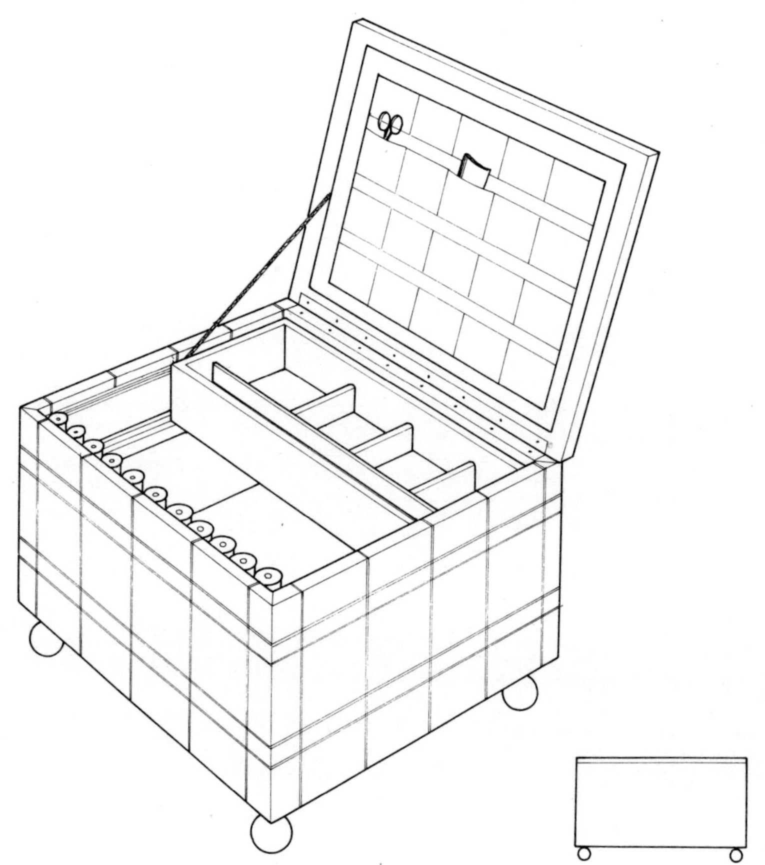

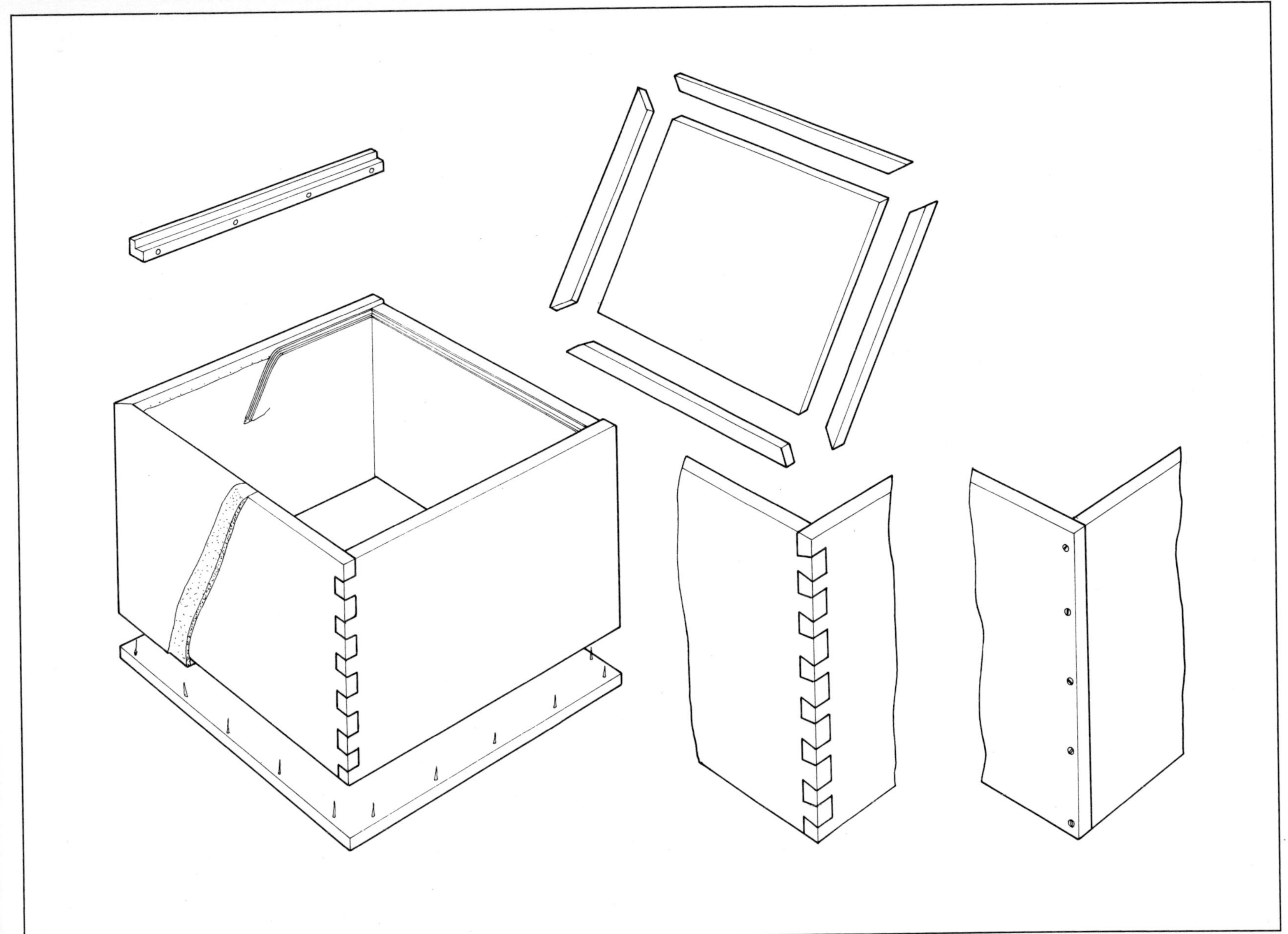

1 Cotton reel racks.

2 Tray partition housing joints.

3 Tray partition glued and nailed and covered in baize.

4 Braid covering the edges of the covering material.

5 Bottom covering material tacked on.

6 Tray runner.

7 Dovetails on tray, partition and run of felt or baize - - - - -.

8 Ply rebated in tray. Partition glued and nailed.

9 Piano hinge set in.

10 Ply covered with material and screwed into recess. Nylon cord secured.

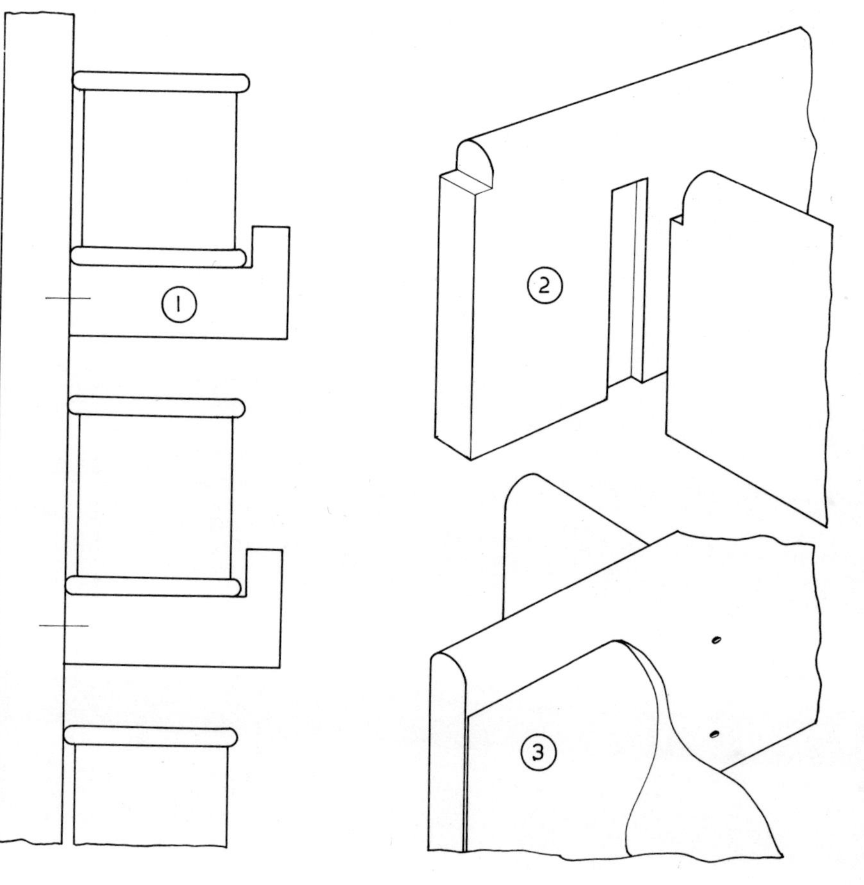

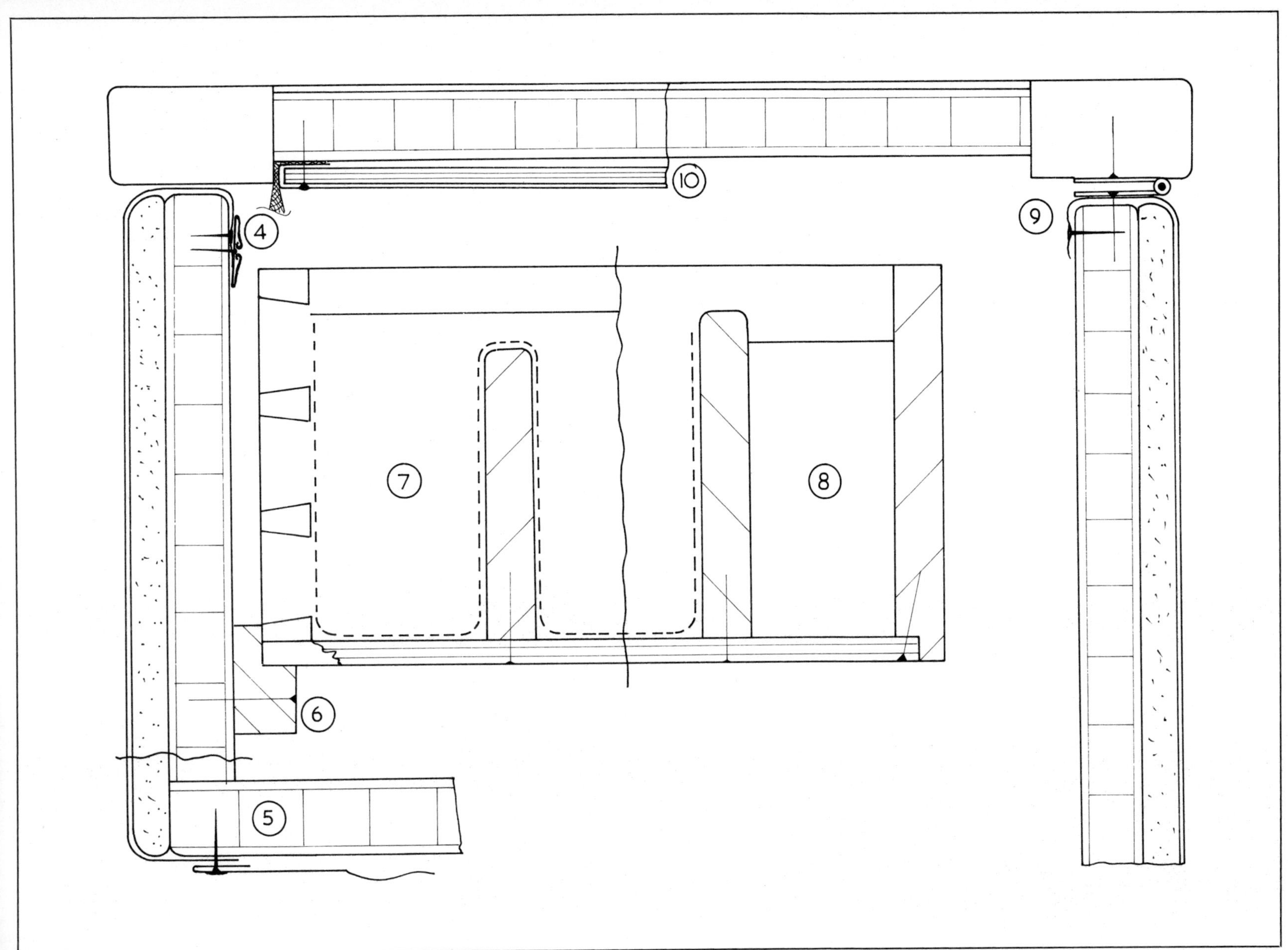
4
5
6
7
8
9
10

11 Ply bottom glued and nailed to sides of box.
$\frac{1}{4}$″ foam spot-glued and tacked on round the
edges. Page 65.
Material stretched round and marked for length.

12 Corner seam sewn (inside out), now turned
right side out and ready for slipping over foam
covered box.

13 Edges tacked down inside and braid applied.

14 Material tacked or stapled to bottom and
covered with cloth (curtain lining).

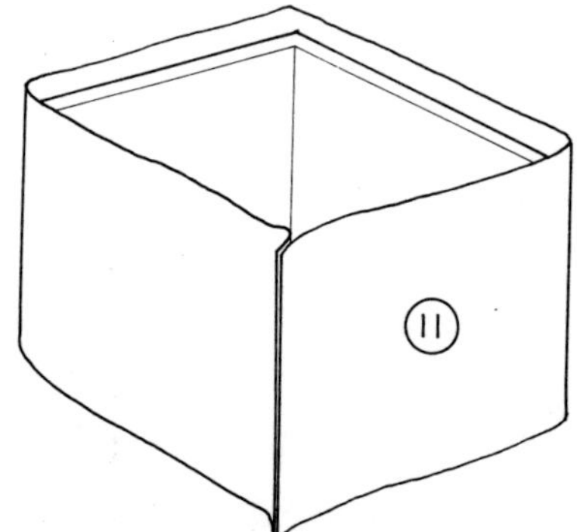

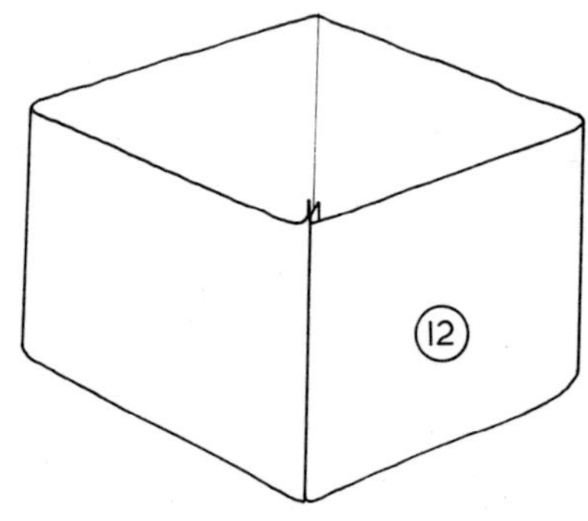

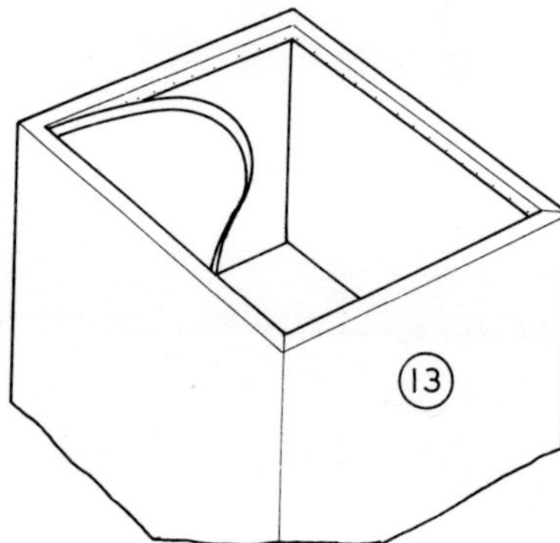

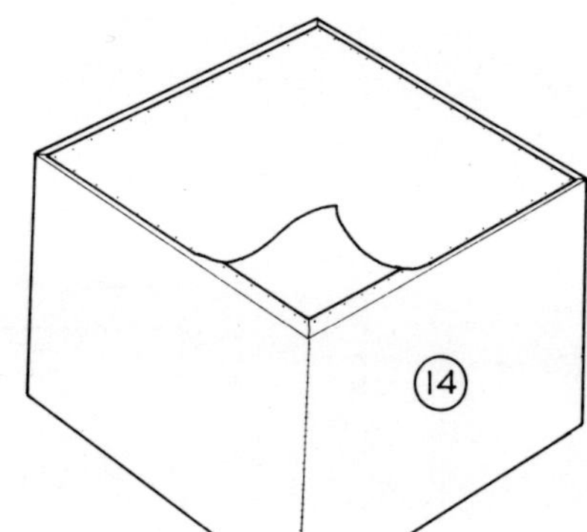

LID PANEL

15 Strips cut and edges sewn.

16 Underside of strip.

17 Strips sewn on cover. A gap may be needed to
allow long-bladed scissors to pass through.

18 Cover stapled to ply panel.

19 Inside of panel.

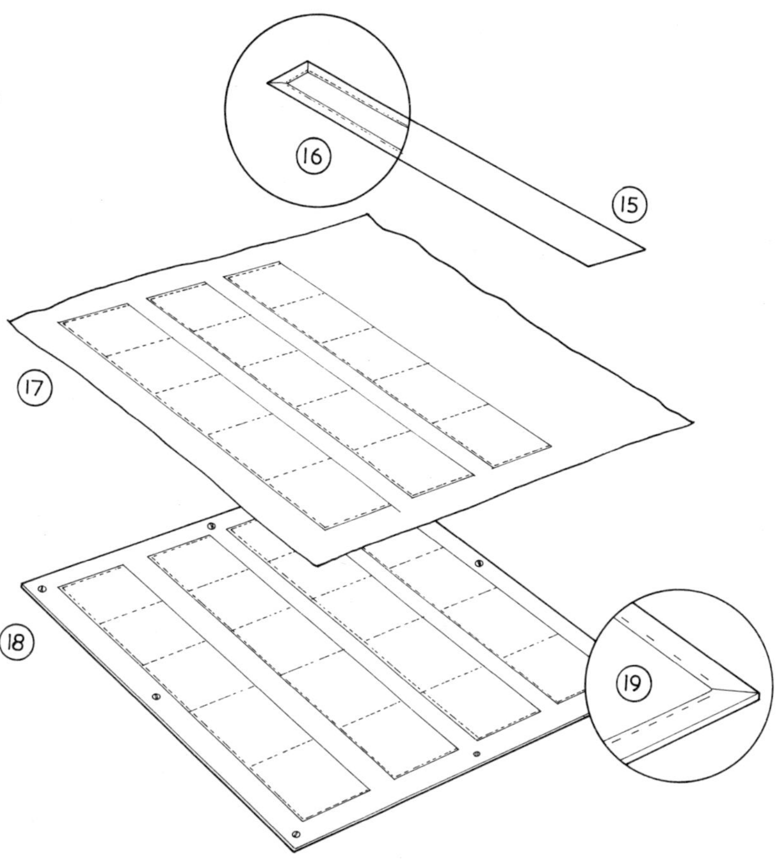

UPHOLSTERED LID

20 Material cut and corners marked for sewing.

21 Corners sewn (inside out).

22 Foam glued to top and cover to be placed over.

23 Material tacked down in recess (inside lid).

24 Panel to be screwed in.

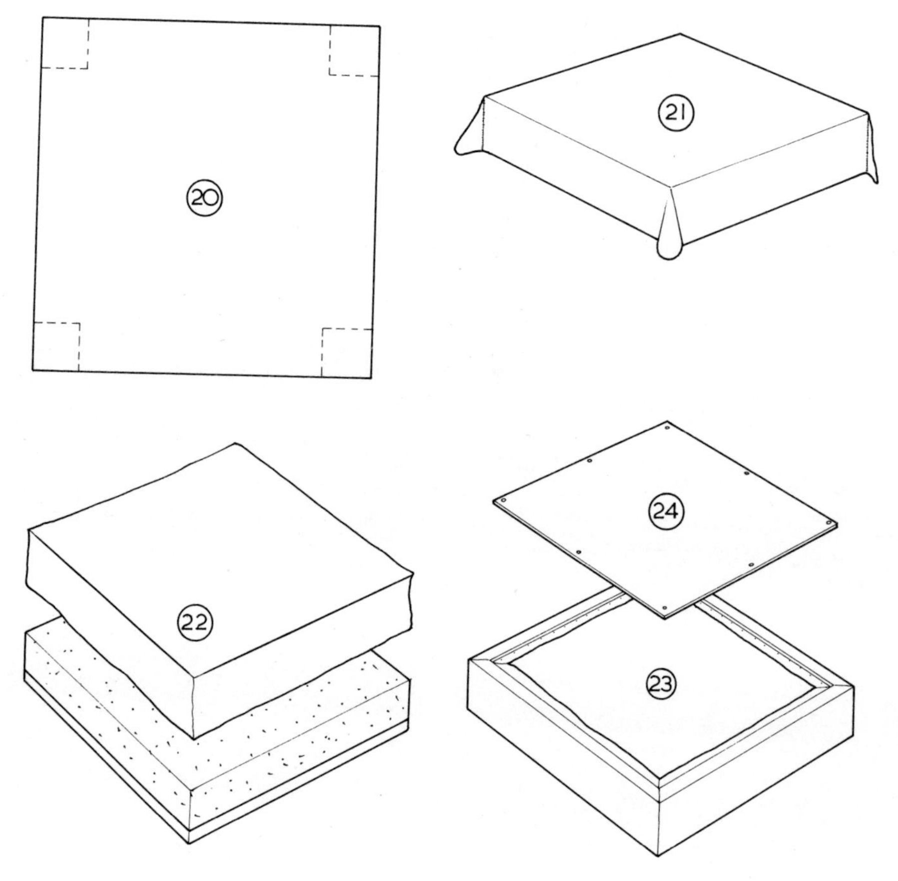

Dressing Table Stool

This stool can be made to match the dressing table, and shapes of end panels can be made accordingly —page 76. $\frac{5}{8}$" blockboard, laminboard or ply can be used for the ends, or frames can be made using mortise and tenon joints. If blockboard is used the edges must be lipped. If ply is used then a filler will be sufficient. The technique for lipping curved edges can be seen on page 39. The frame supporting the ply seat can be dowelled or mortised and tenoned together.

The stool can be about 18" high to the top of the foam, which can be 2"–3" thick and quite firm (some foams are too soft). The width can be 16"–20" and the depth 12"–15". Draw it full size and use a chair to test your measurements. The ply seat can be glued and pinned to the seat frame, which can be bolted or screwed or dowelled to the sides—page 21. The sides can be painted with polyurethane and the rails left natural or all parts painted or veneered—page 89.

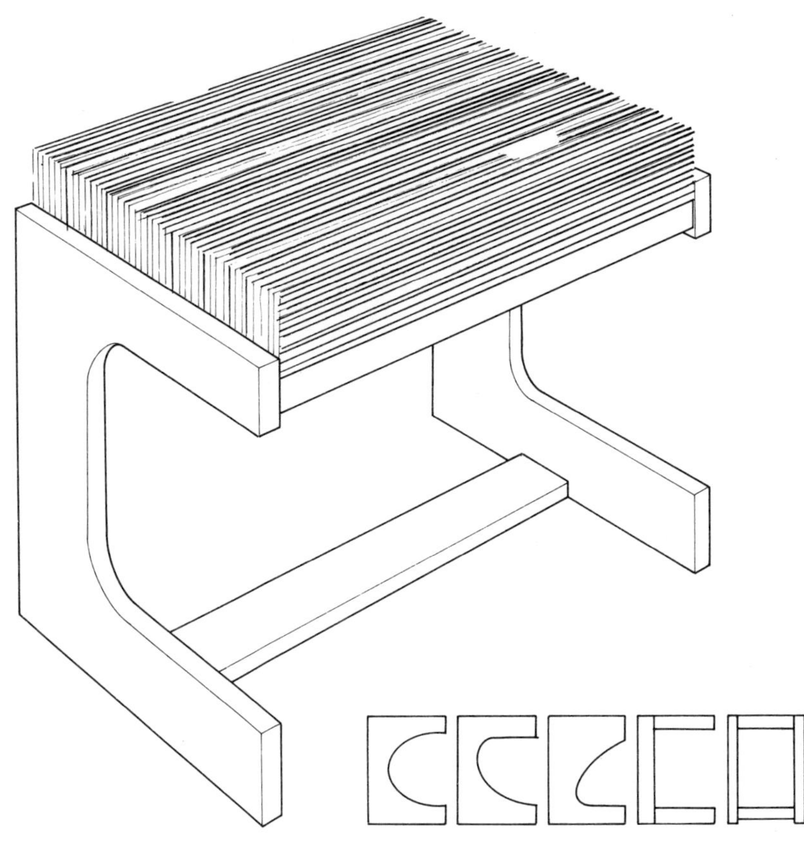

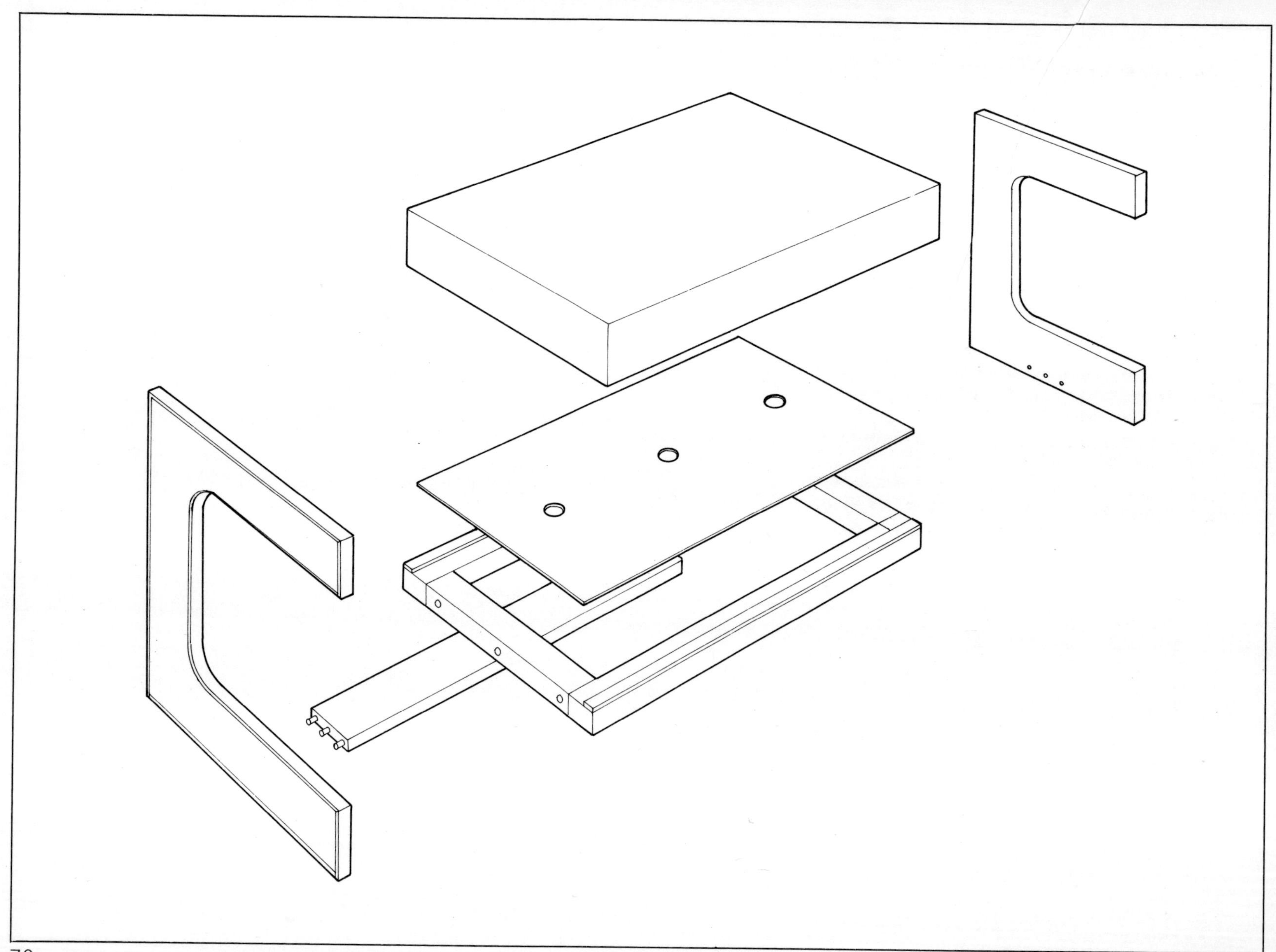

Try this with paper until you are used to the method.

1 Pattern for cutting out.

2 Sew corners—inside out.

3 Trim corners. Sew ends to bottom—inside out.

4 Sew ends to leave an opening—inside out.

5 Complete sewing ends to bottom—inside out.

6 Sew in one side of zip—inside out.

7 Open the zip and sew in the second side of the zip—inside out.

8 Turn to right side. Insert foam cushion.

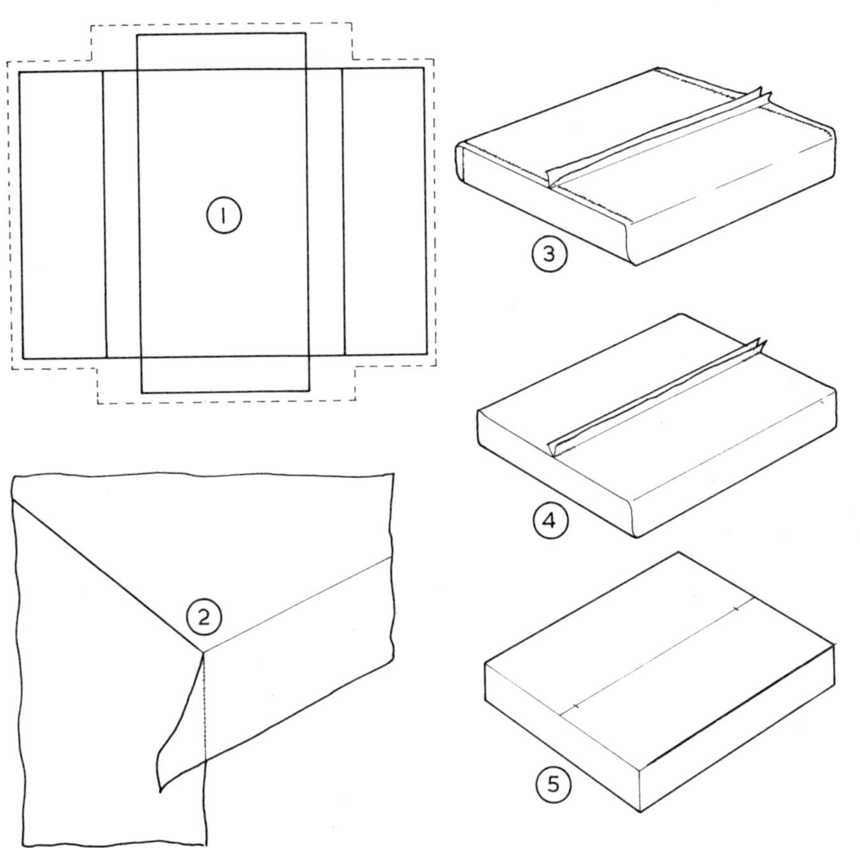

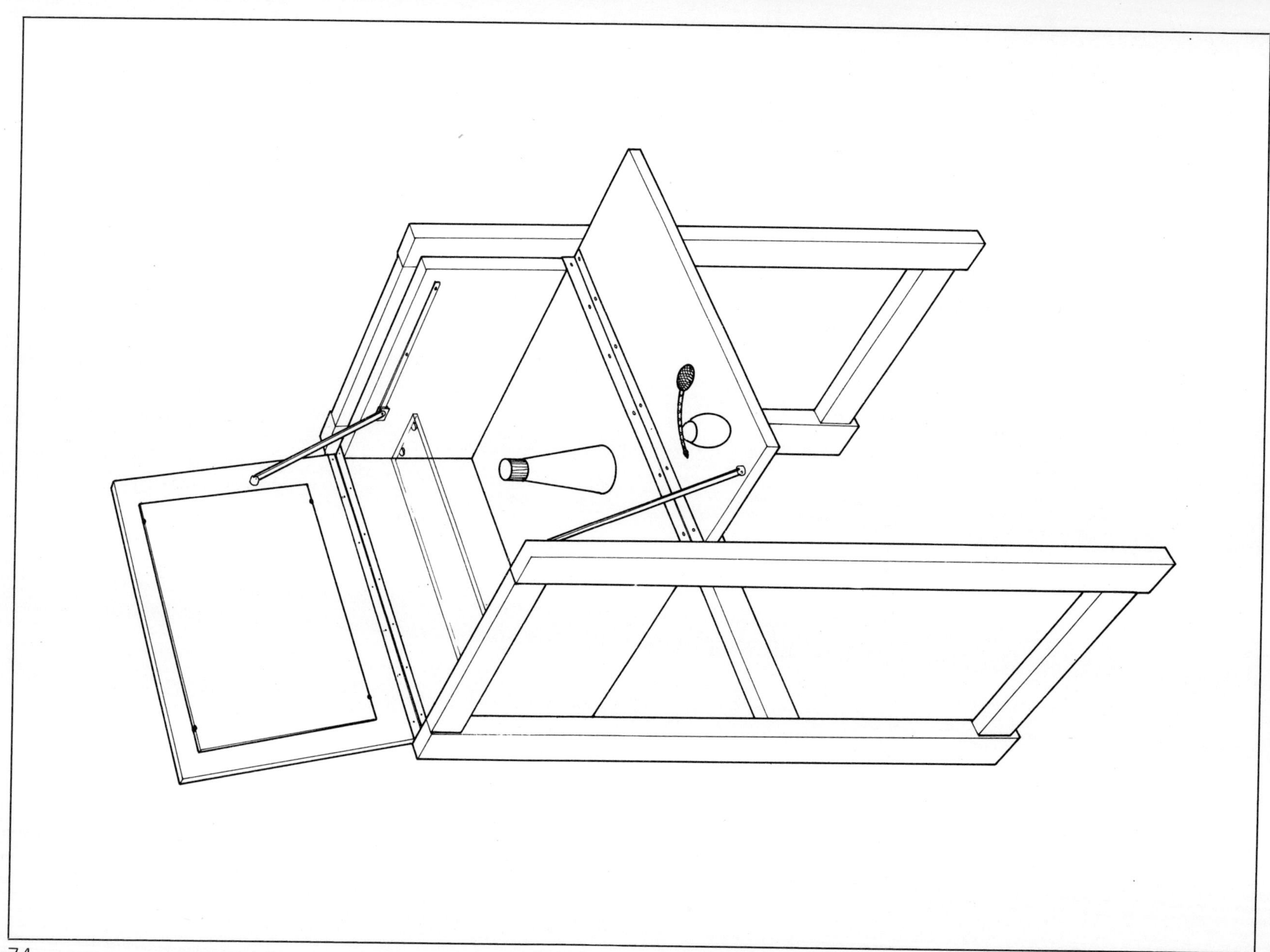

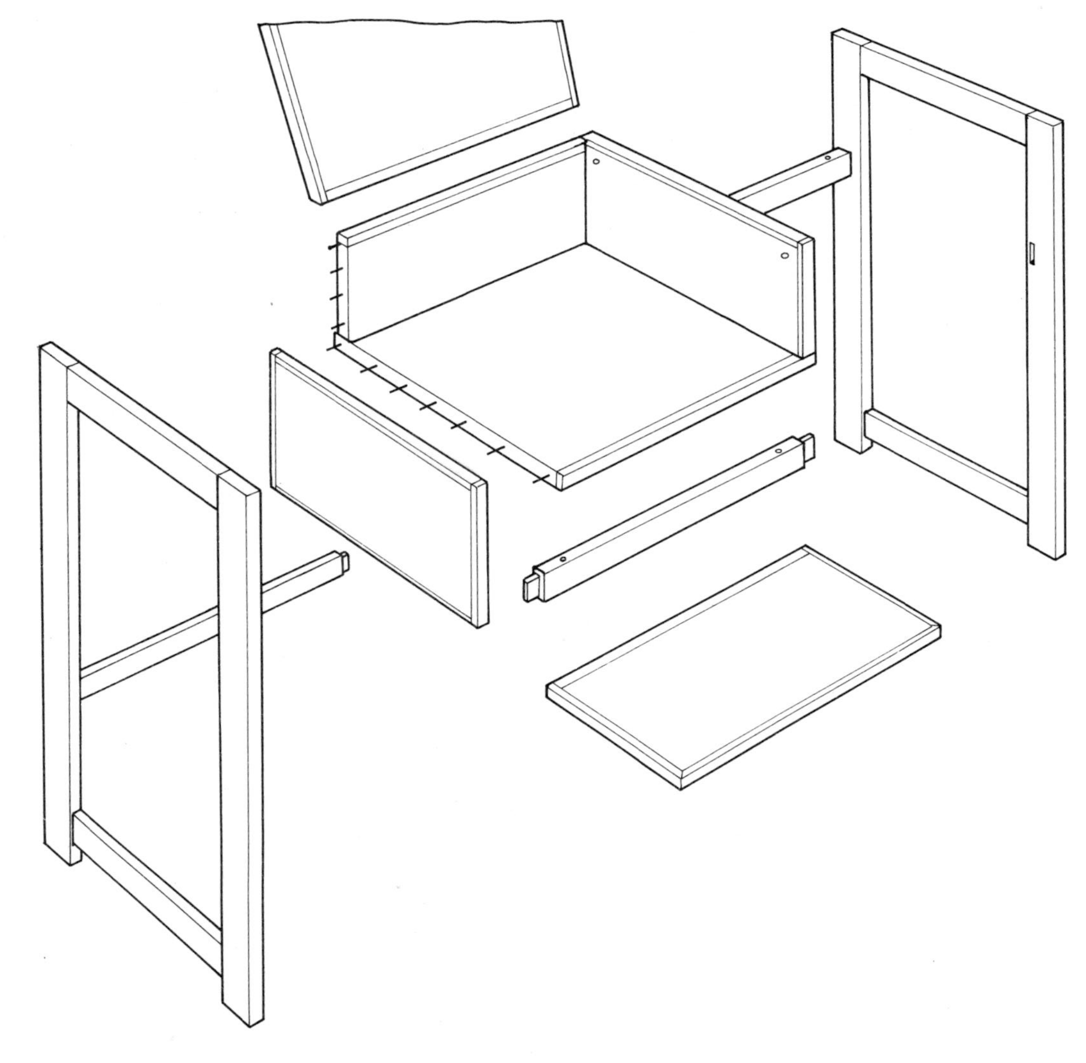

Dressing Table

This dressing table can be made sufficiently wide to allow the stool—page 71—to pass easily underneath so that the inside measurement of the table should be 2"–3" wider than the outside measurement of the stool.

The fall front can be about 24" from the floor and the depth of the box should be based on the heights of bottles and jars to be stored—8" should be sufficient. It is useful to draw a full-size elevation of the box and the outer frames—pages

76, 77—to decide on final measurements. The box is made from $\frac{5}{8}$" blockboard which is lipped with solid wood where necessary.

The inside surface can be veneered or painted with polyurethane or faced, especially on the bottom and the fall, with plastic laminate (do not apply to the position of the piano hinge). The outside of the box can be veneered or painted or covered in plastic laminate. Stays will be required for fall and lid. A $\frac{1}{4}$" plate glass shelf can be supported on white or brown plastic shelf fittings. A small $\frac{3}{16}$" mirror can be secured to the inside of the fall with edge or corner clips. The side panels can be made from $\frac{5}{8}$" blockboard, or framed by using mortise and tenon joints. Various forms of panels are shown.

Section through box.

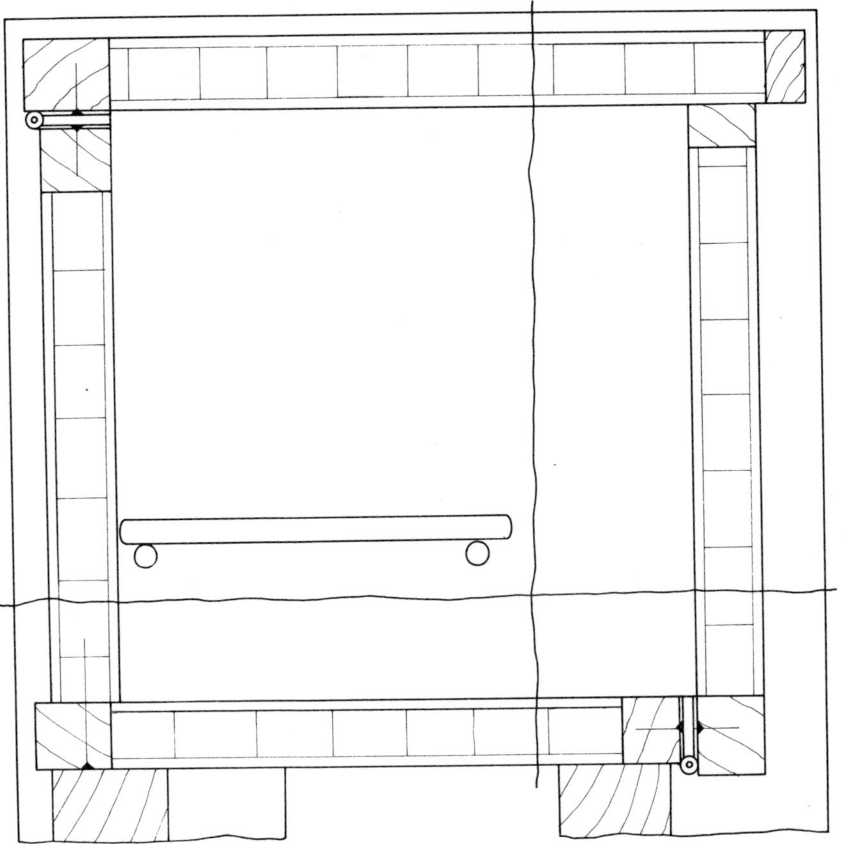

Writing and Dressing Table

This fitment offers a satisfactory solution to a problem which is often very difficult to solve. It is designed to fit in the corner of a bedroom which is too small for traditional-free standing pieces of furniture. Apart from one leg—which can easily be removed by gently lifting the table—there is an uninterrupted floor space for cleaning or carpet laying. One chair can be used for both purposes, which again is a saving of space and money. The height of the table can be about 28″–29″ and the depth of the drawer about 3″, otherwise it will be difficult to get one's knees under. Alternatively if the drawer is not fitted then the height of the table can be 26″ or even 25″, which is a very good working height for writing, drawing and typing. The table top can be made from $\frac{3}{4}$″ blockboard and the unit from $\frac{5}{8}$″ blockboard or solid wood. The drawer is made from $\frac{3}{8}$″ material with a laid-on front, the bottom edge of which can serve as a handle. The mirror can be of standard size and secured to the wall by fittings which allow an air space behind. This can be an advantage in the case of an outside wall where there might be slight dampness.

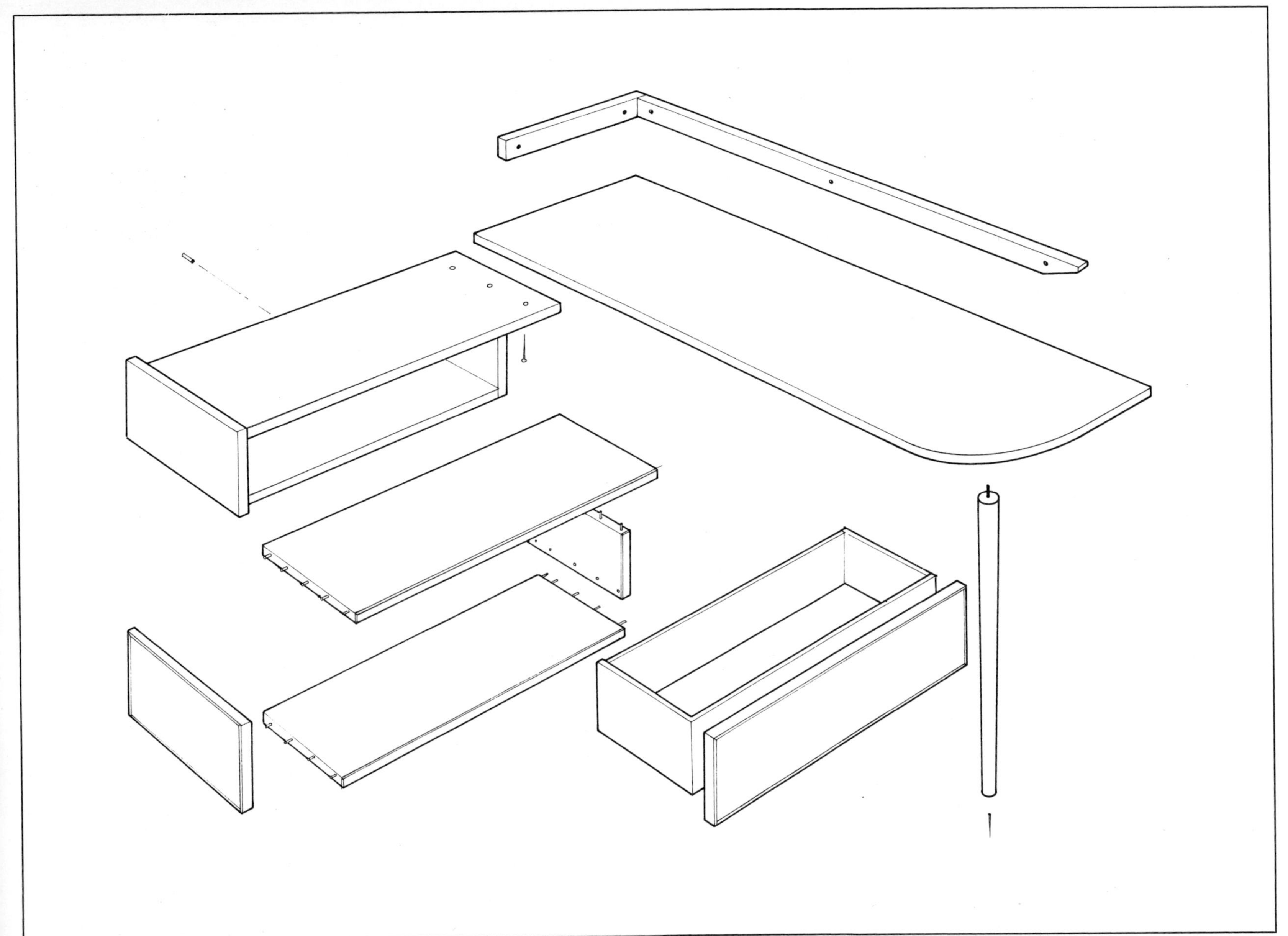

TOP

1 Lipped for paint or lacquer finish.

2 Edge and surface faced with plastic laminate—
The radius must be large—test.

3 Edge lipped and surface veneered.

4 Applying the laminate to the side of the drawer
unit in the order A, B, C.

5 Screw fixed into wall (head removed). Drawer
unit is now pushed on. The other end of the unit
is screwed to the underside of the table.

6 The leg is located on a dowel at the top and a
screw (head removed) at the bottom.

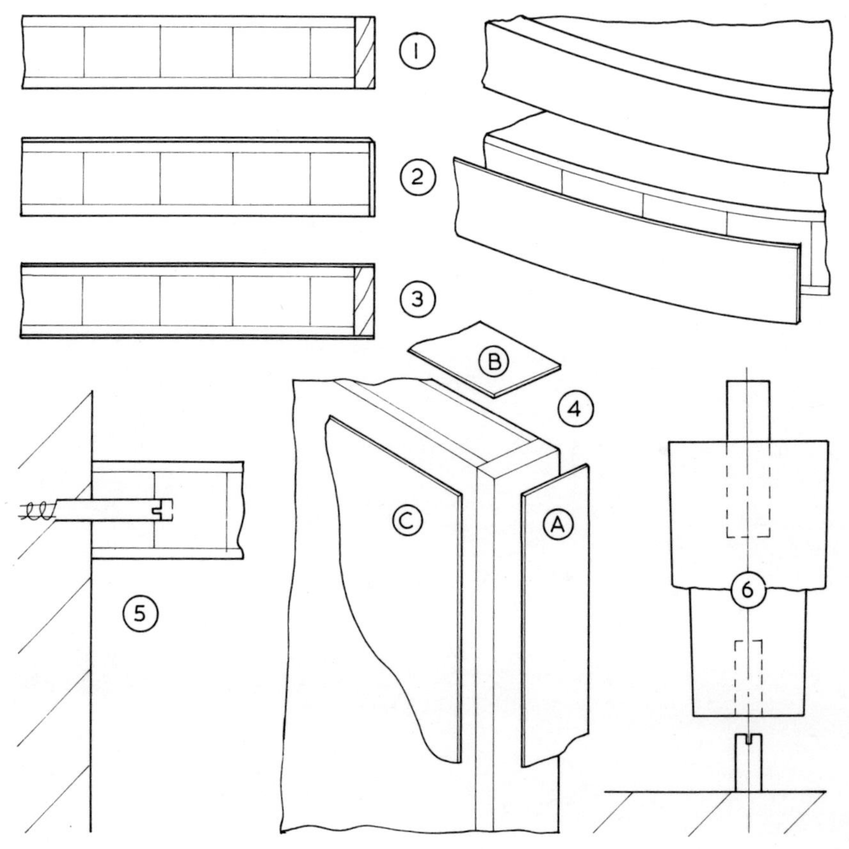

Section through dressing table unit showing :

  7 Drawer side (back).

  8 Drawer side with ply in groove.

  9 Drawer side (front).

10 Laid-on front.

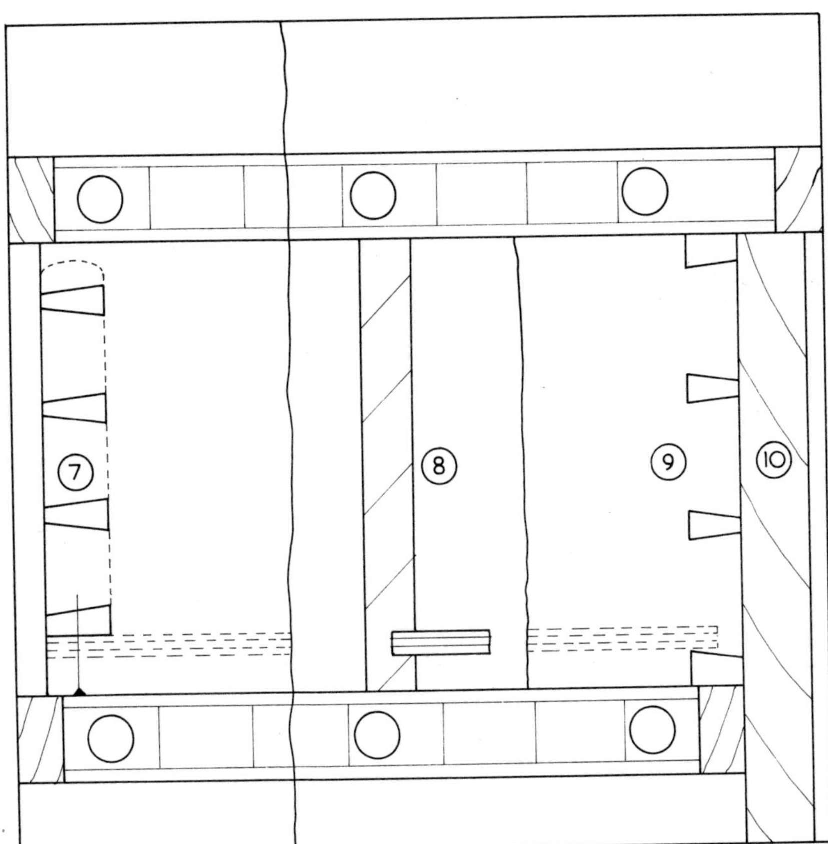

Writing Desk

This item combines several useful features. There is an uninterrupted leg space which allows the desk top to be as low as 26". The box at the rear provides ample storage for files, and, if required, a drawing board can be stored between two guides under the top. The top can be made from $\frac{3}{4}$" blockboard which can be lipped and veneered or covered in plastic laminate. It can also be covered in lino and then lipped—page 49. The surface of the lid of the filing cabinet can be polished wood to form a contrast with the desk top.

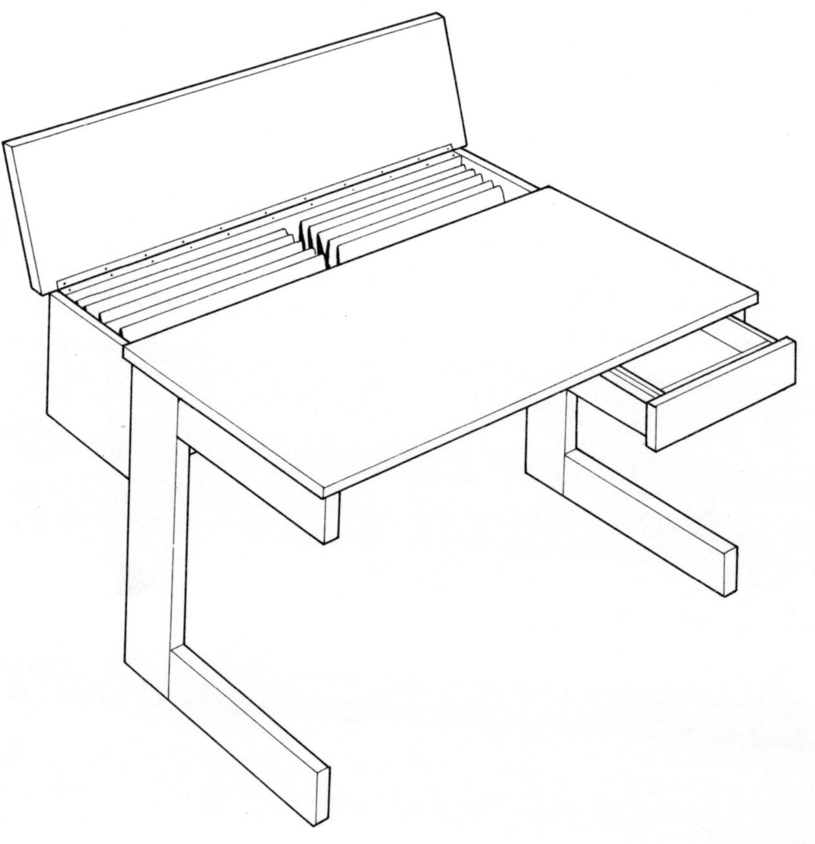

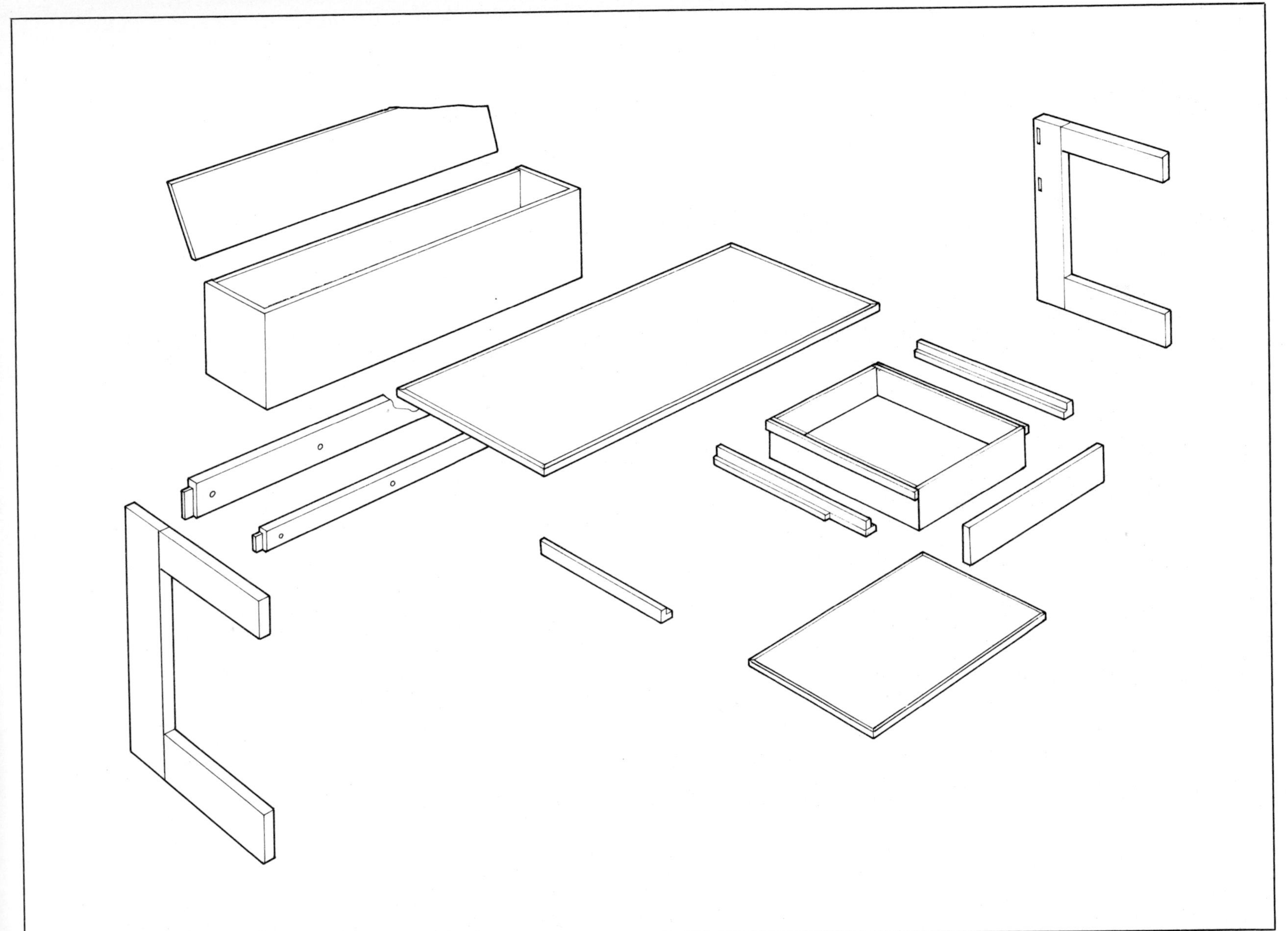

The side frames can be made from 4″ × $\frac{7}{8}$″ or 1″ material using 2$\frac{1}{2}$″ × $\frac{1}{2}$″ dia. dowels or mortise and tenon joints. The two frames are joined together by two back rails to which the filing cabinet is secured, making a common level between the desk and the cabinet lid. The cabinet sides can be made from $\frac{5}{8}$″ × 11″ board dovetailed at the corners. $\frac{1}{2}$″ blockboard can be rebated or loose tongued into the bottom. The lid can be lipped $\frac{5}{8}$″ block-board. A piano hinge will give a good movement which can be stopped with a jointed stay or nylon cord—page 60.

The drawer is made from $\frac{3}{8}$″ material and the front is glued on to provide a handle at the lower edge. Two extra pieces of wood are glued to the drawer sides and these slide between guides glued and screwed to the underside of the desk top.

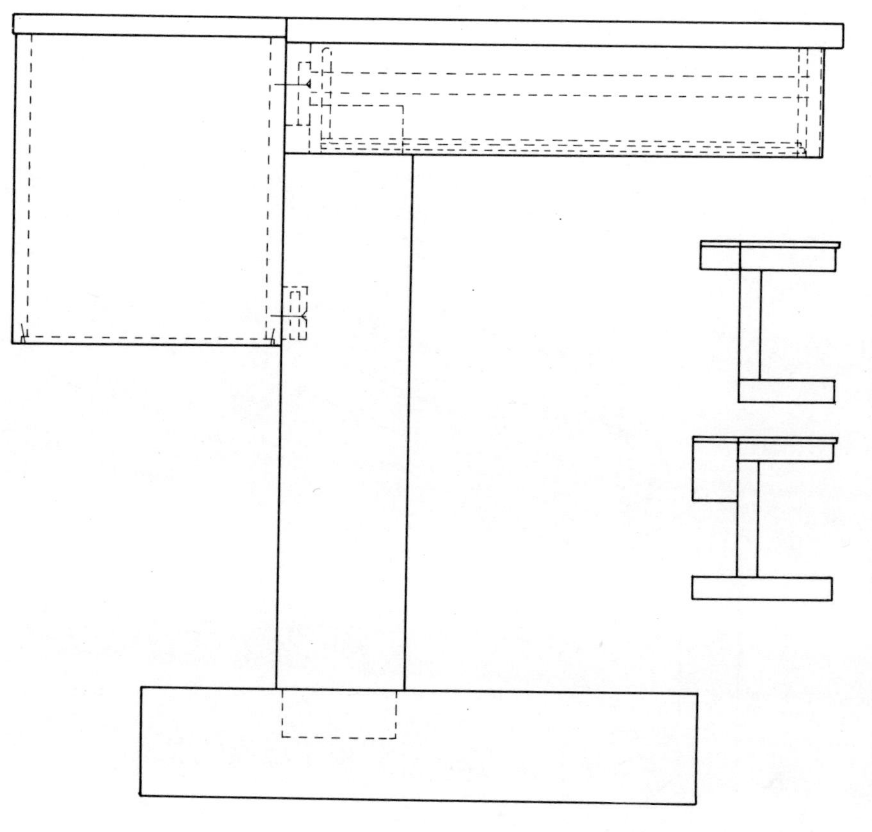

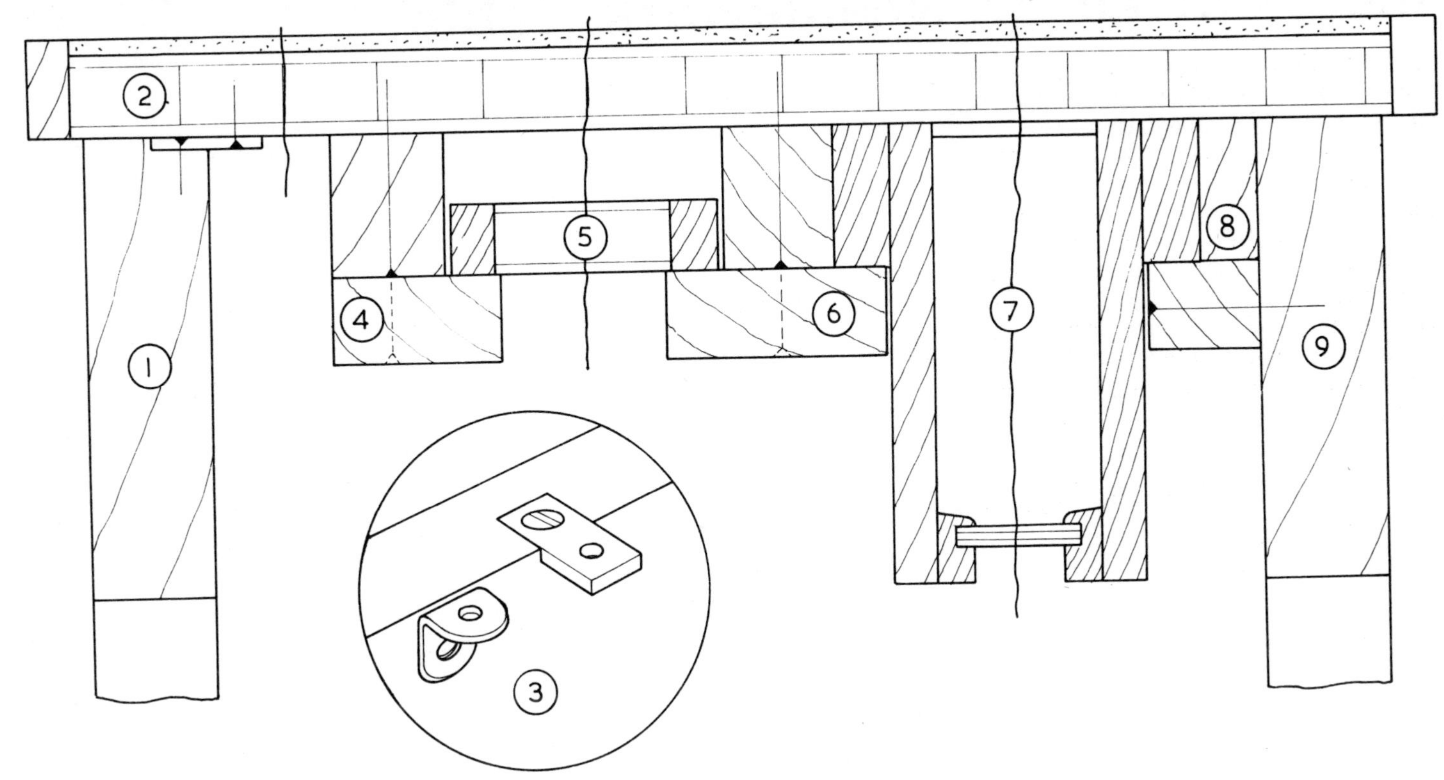

SECTIONS

1 Side frame.

2 Top of blockboard faced with lino and lipped with $\frac{3}{8}$″ material.

3 Top joined to frame by plates.

4 Drawing board runner.

5 Drawing board.

6 Runner for drawing board and drawer.

7 Drawer sides, slips and ply bottom.

8 Drawer runner.

9 Side frame.

Games, Coffee or Needlework Table

This table is made with a lipped and veneered $\frac{5}{8}$" blockboard top. One side is plain veneered and the other side is squared for chess or draughts. The well can be used for storage of games, magazines or needlework. The table can be made 20"–24" square and about 15" high. The legs can be $1\frac{5}{8}$"–2" square and the sides between 4"–6" wide. The bottom can be made from $\frac{1}{4}$" ply, or greater stiffness may be obtained from $\frac{1}{2}$" blockboard. A bottom lining of brightly coloured baize or felt can be glued in after the main frame has been assembled. Resin W adhesive can be applied to the ply or blockboard and the felt secured. If the adjacent edges of the felt are cut, then the over-hang on the other two sides can be trimmed off when in position by cutting against a 6" or 12" ruler pressed well into the corners.

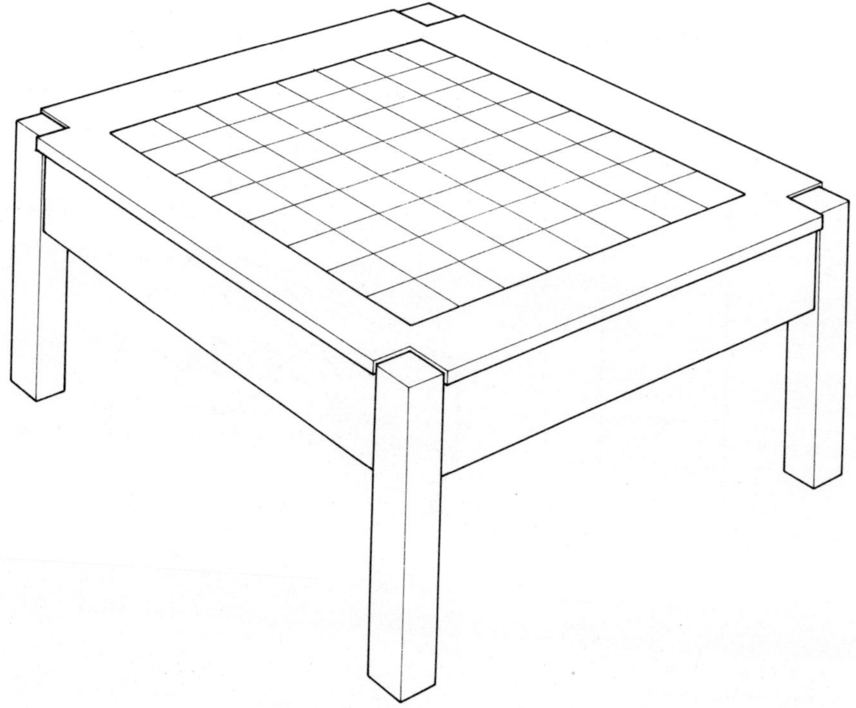

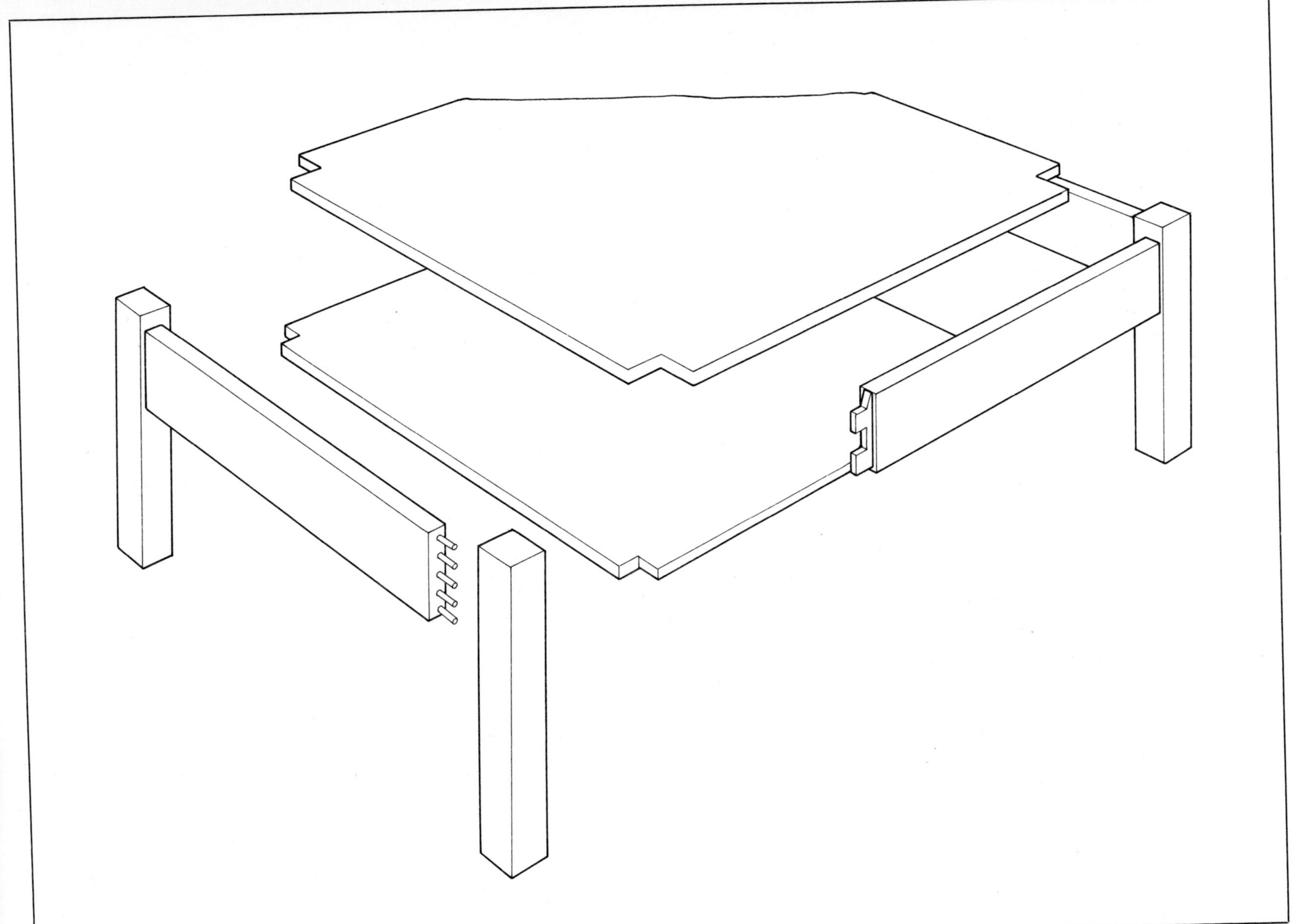

The squared surface is made from veneers which
are cut a little wider and longer than required and
are then placed between two 1″ thick battens that
have been screwed or bolted together and planed
parallel. The projecting edges of the veneers are
then planed down level with the battens with a very
sharp finely set 15″ steel plane. These strips are
now removed and taped together (1″ gummed
strip)—alternate light and dark. Strips are now cut
across the grain, leaving a small allowance for a
second planing operation between the wooden
battens.

1 Blockboard cut (with allowances for lipping) to
   fit round legs.

2 Corner lippings glued on using Resin W adhesive.

3 Side lippings glued on.

4 Four strips of dark veneer and four strips of light
   veneer cut for planing to width.

5 1″ thick wooden bars screwed or bolted
   together for planing veneers to width.

6 Alternate strips of light and dark veneer gum-
   taped together (thin tape).

7 Cross cutting strips to form squares—steel bar.

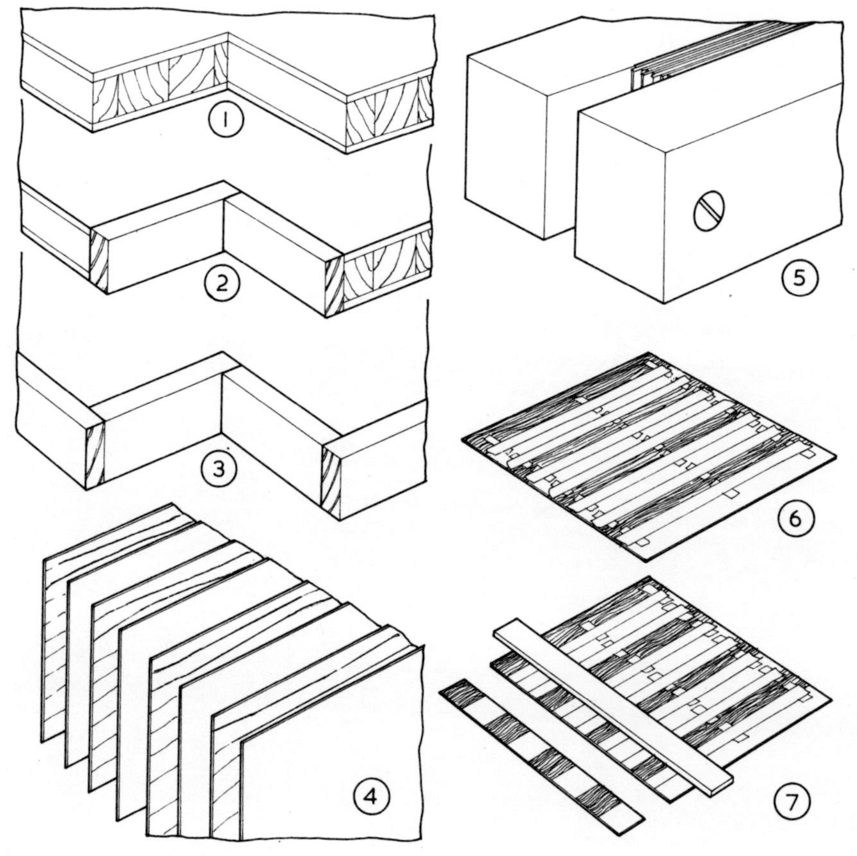

This time care must be taken to prevent the ends from breaking out whilst planing. The strips are again removed and taped together to form alternate squares of light and dark veneers. The outline of the large square should now be pencilled in on the blockboard and the surface glued, using a formaldehyde type of adhesive. The squares are now secured with Sellotape to prevent slipping while pressure is being applied with twelve deep-throated G cramps on two pieces of $1\frac{1}{4}$" thick blockboard ($\frac{5}{8}$" pieces glued together). To prevent the squares from becoming glued to the wooden platten it is advisable to cover the squares with paper or a metal platten. Ten minutes should now elapse before releasing the top platten to clean off the glue with a 1" chisel and a damp rag. This saves a lot of time at a later stage. The pressure must now be restored until the glue has set, when the two opposite borders can be fitted, taped into position and glued as with the squares. When the glue is set the remaining borders can be planed and fitted, taped and cramped as previously.

8 Planing veneers to width to form squares.

9 Strips of squares taped together (shown without tape).

10 Squares glued and Sellotaped to $\frac{5}{8}$" blockboard.

11 Cramped between plattens or in veneer press.

12 Borders of veneer fitted, glued and Sellotaped, before being placed under pressure.

13 Opposite borders of veneer prepared for pressing.

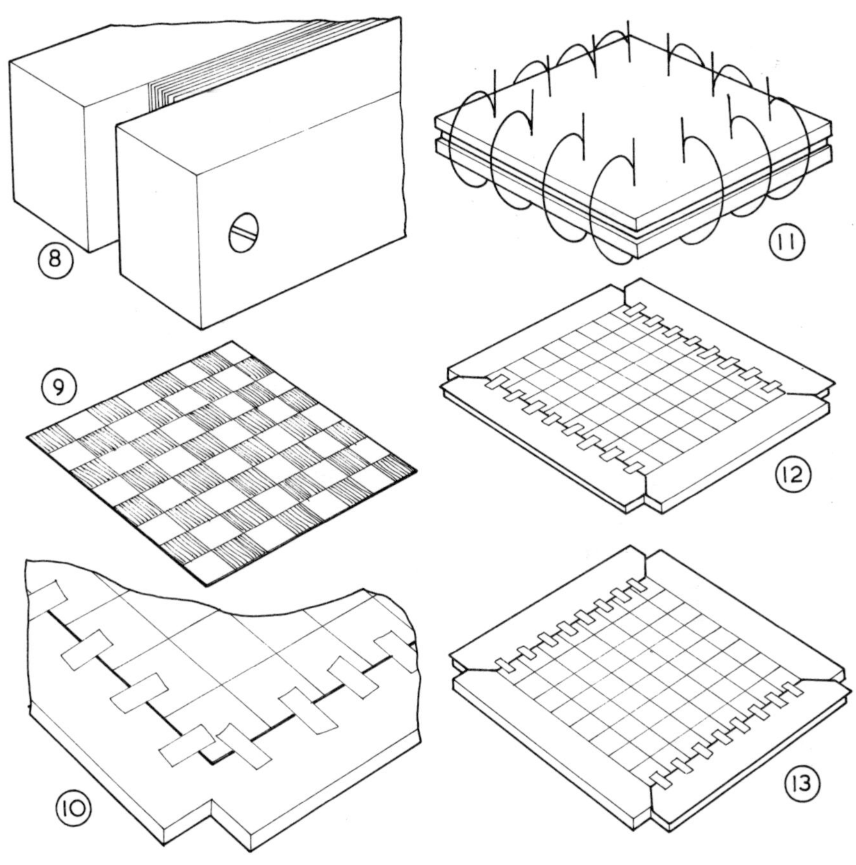

The other side of the top can be veneered using
the same type of glue, paper, wooden plattens and
G cramps. A veneer press will make these operations
easier.
It is possible to attach the borders so that the whole
of the squared surface can be glued in one
operation, but great care would be needed to
prevent slip, as adjustment at the mitres would then
be impossible.
Gummed tape can be softened with a damp rag and
then peeled off. Final cleaning can be done with a
cabinet scraper and garnet paper.
Finish : lacquer on legs and top. Rails painted.
    or lacquer on legs, rails and top.
    or lacquer on top. Legs and rails painted.
    or lacquer on legs and top. Rails covered with
    P.V.C.

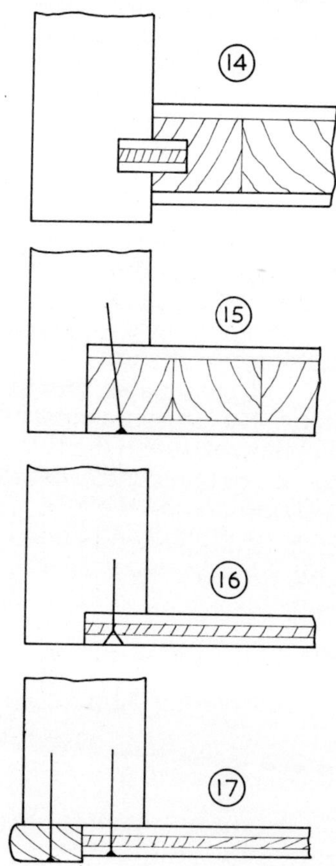

14 $\frac{1}{2}$" blockboard secured with $\frac{1}{2}$" wide loose
     tongue.

15 $\frac{1}{2}$" blockboard in rebate. Glued and pinned.

16 Ply in rebate.

17 Ply nailed and glued. Beading nailed and
     glued.

Opposite page shows some CHESS MEN.

Sideboard

The height of a sideboard is often about table height so that transfer is easy between the two surfaces. If the cabinet is to be made with shelves a cabinet height of 18″ would be useful, although the items to be stored should be considered and the cabinet designed accordingly. The length can be as required. For a 3′ cabinet the lower rails can be about 2″ × 1″ but for a 6′ cabinet (with extra doors) the lower rails can be about 3″ × $1\frac{1}{4}$″. The cabinet can be made from 15″–22″ in width depending on the items to be stored.

The main surfaces of the cabinet are made from $\frac{5}{8}$″ blockboard, laminboard or plywood. The ends are only lipped on the front edges. The top edges are required for dovetailing and the back edges are covered in ply. The legs of 1″ thick material are glued directly on to the ends using Resin W adhesive. An actual gluing surface of 2″ width will produce a strong bond. The bottom is dowelled ($\frac{5}{16}$″ dia.) into the sides and the under rails are mortised into the legs at the back and the front.

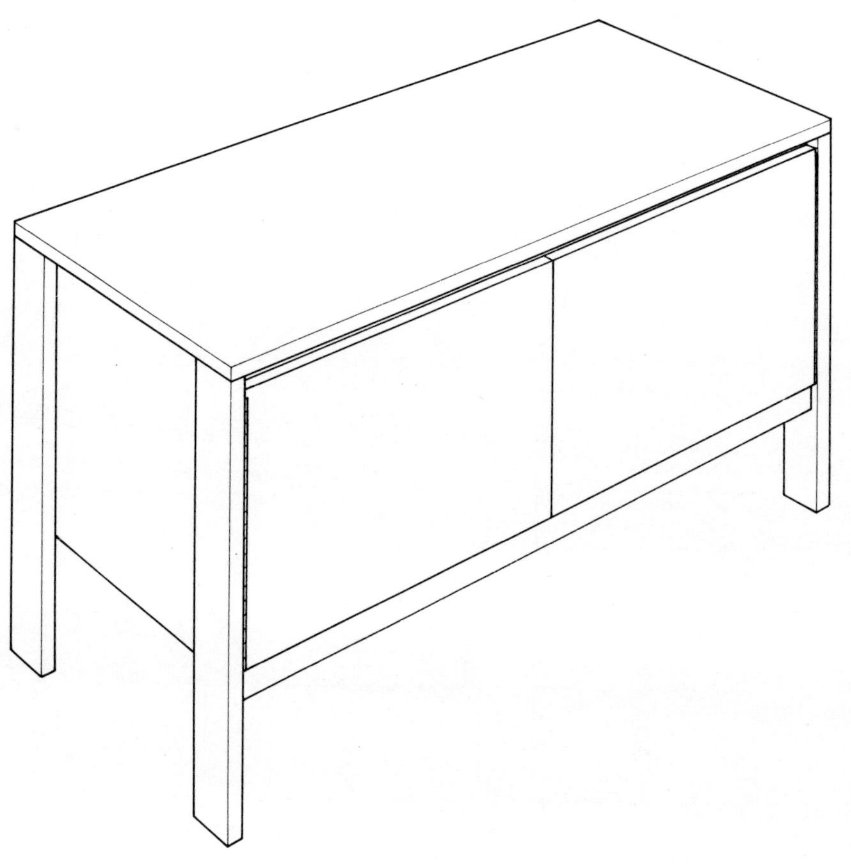

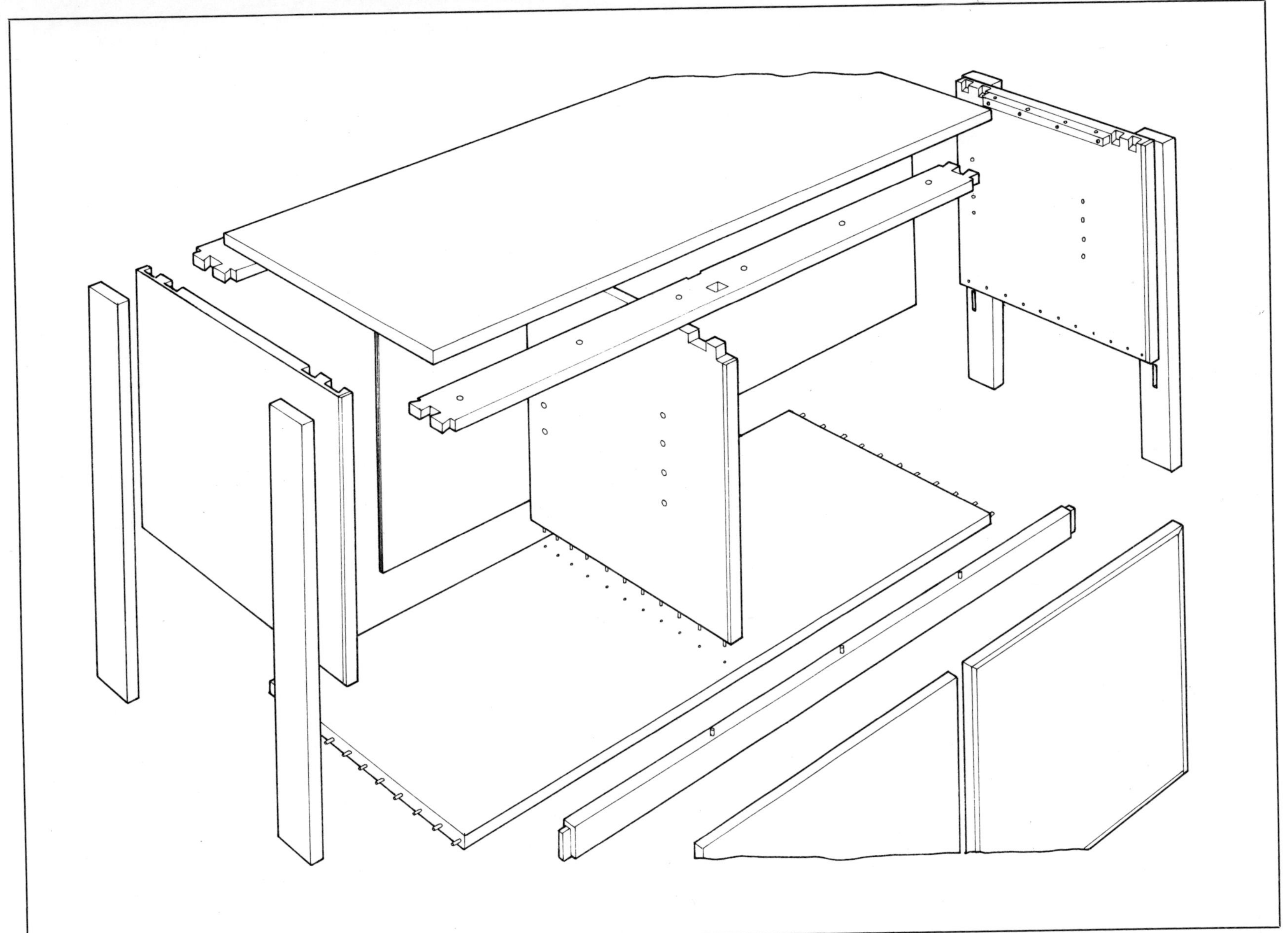

The $\frac{7}{8}$" thick top rails are dovetailed into the board and for this purpose the blocks of the board must run vertically. Large dovetails and pins (about $1\frac{1}{8}$") must be cut to prevent the pins from breaking down. A $\frac{3}{16}$" lap will leave sufficient strength in the board.

All surfaces can be veneered if a veneer press is available; otherwise the ends and doors can be painted with polyurethane and the top can be made from standard veneered board or blockboard covered with plastic laminate.

1 Top of carcase showing part of leg, rail and ply back.

2 Top front corner of carcase showing leg, front rail and door.

3 Section through top of carcase, top rail, door and door opening aperture.

4 Section through bottom of carcase, lower front rail and door.

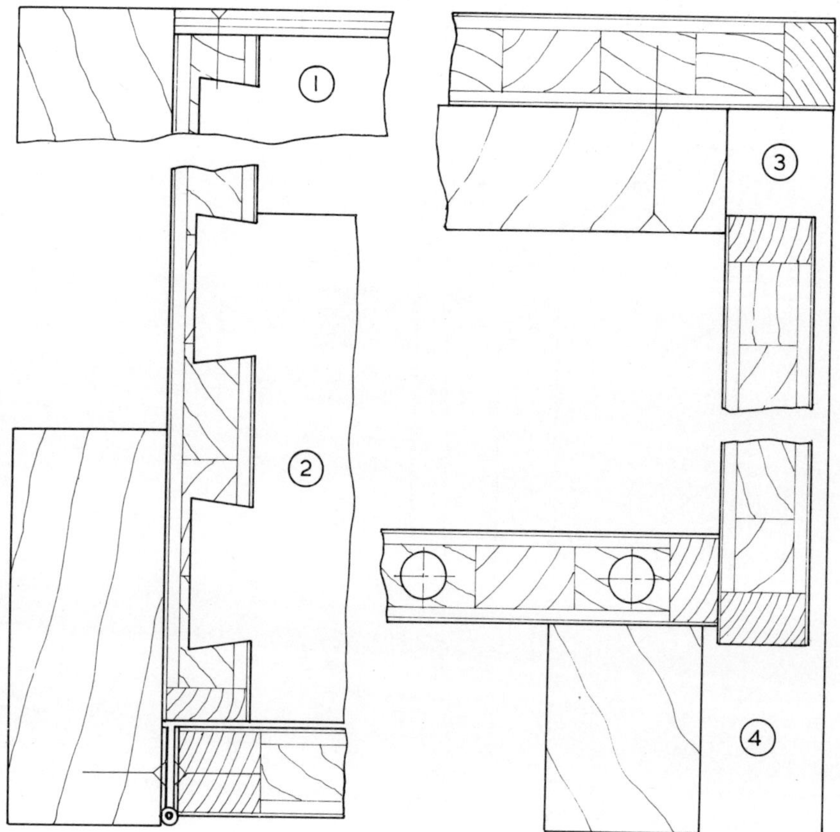

The technique of securing the laminate (without
a press) is to use a contact adhesive and give a
quick but firm pressure on the surface near the
edges. Apply this pressure with a 3" engineer's
vice or G cramp, using fairly thick batten to
distribute the pressure evenly. The ends and doors
can also be covered with P.V.C. cloth, in which
case, after gluing the cloth to the door fronts, the
lipping can be applied to the door edges to protect
the cloth. Ready veneered blockboard can also be
used throughout. The top is secured through the
rails. Shelves can be made from $\frac{1}{2}$" blockboard and
may be adjusted for height on white or brown
plastic shelf fittings.

5 Door hinged on to front of leg.

6 Door hinged on inside of leg.

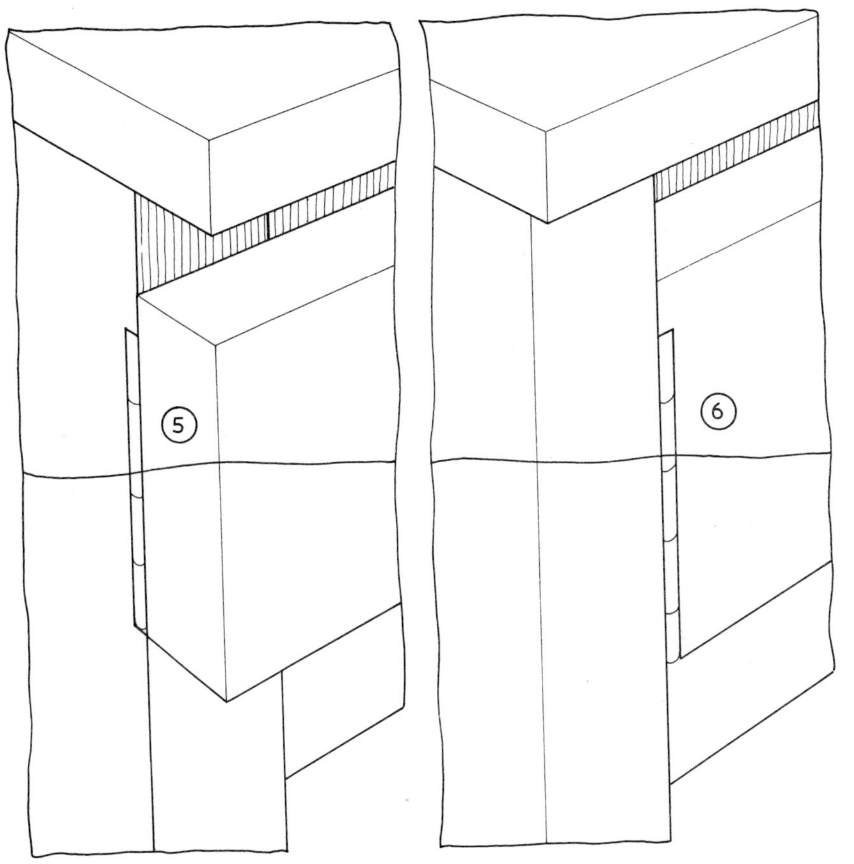